THEOLOGICAL ERRORS IN THE QURAN

Dr. Maxwell Shimba

Shimba Publishing, LLC
Printed in the United States of America

First Printing Edition 2024

TABLE OF CONTENTS

THE DIFFERENCE BETWEEN ISLAMIC AND CHRISTIAN THEOLOGIES

The study of theology reveals profound insights into the core beliefs, doctrines, and practices that define different faith traditions. Christianity and Islam, two of the world's major religions, provide rich theological landscapes that have shaped human history and continue to influence billions of adherents. This chapter explores the critical differences between Islamic and Christian theologies, delving into their distinct views on the nature of God, Jesus Christ, holy scriptures, salvation, prophets, sin, religious practices, the role of religious leaders, eschatology, and their perspectives on other religions.

The Nature of God

Christianity: The Trinity

At the heart of Christian theology is the doctrine of the Trinity, which posits that God exists as one essence in three persons: the Father, the Son (Jesus Christ), and the Holy Spirit. This triune nature of God is a cornerstone of Christian belief, emphasizing both the unity and co-equality of the three persons. The Nicene Creed, formulated in the fourth century, encapsulates this doctrine, affirming that the Father, Son, and Holy Spirit are of the same substance (homoousios) and equally divine.

Islam: Tawhid

Islamic theology, on the other hand, is grounded in the principle of Tawhid, the absolute oneness and indivisibility of God (Allah). The Shahada, the Islamic declaration of faith, states, "There is no god but Allah, and Muhammad is his messenger," underscoring the monotheistic essence of Islam. The concept of the Trinity is firmly rejected in Islam, and associating partners with Allah (shirk) is considered the gravest sin.

Jesus Christ

Christianity: Divine Savior

In Christianity, Jesus Christ is central as the Son of God, the second person of the Trinity. Christians believe in his incarnation, where God became fully human while remaining fully divine. The crucifixion, death, and resurrection of Jesus are foundational events that provide the basis for human salvation. Christians hold that Jesus' sacrifice on the cross atoned for the sins of humanity, offering eternal life to those who believe in him.

Islam: Esteemed Prophet

Islam acknowledges Jesus (Isa) as one of the greatest prophets but not divine. The Quran teaches that Jesus was born of the Virgin Mary, performed miracles, and will return at the end of times. However, Islam rejects the crucifixion, asserting instead that Jesus was not killed but was raised to heaven by Allah. Jesus is highly respected, but his role is seen as a precursor to Muhammad, the final prophet.

Holy Scriptures

Christianity: The Bible

The Christian holy scripture is the Bible, composed of the Old Testament and the New Testament. The Old Testament includes texts sacred to Judaism, while the New Testament contains writings specific to Christianity, detailing the life, teachings, death, and resurrection of Jesus Christ. Christians believe the Bible is divinely inspired and authoritative for faith and practice.

Islam: The Quran

Islam's sacred text is the Quran, believed to be the literal word of God as revealed to Muhammad by the angel Gabriel. The Quran is considered infallible and the ultimate source of guidance. In addition to the Quran, the Hadith—collections of sayings and actions of Muhammad—plays a crucial role in Islamic theology and jurisprudence.

Salvation

Christianity: Grace through Faith

Christian theology teaches that salvation is a gift of God's grace, received through faith in Jesus Christ. The apostle Paul emphasizes in his letters that it is not by works but by grace that believers are saved (Ephesians 2:8-9). This grace is made possible through Jesus' sacrificial death and resurrection, which atones for sin and reconciles humanity to God.

Islam: Submission and Deeds

In Islam, salvation is achieved through submission to the will of Allah and adherence to the Five Pillars of Islam: Shahada (faith declaration), Salah (prayer), Zakat (charity), Sawm (fasting during Ramadan), and Hajj (pilgrimage to Mecca). While Allah's mercy is paramount, good deeds and observance of Islamic law (Sharia) are essential for attaining paradise.

Prophets and Revelation

Christianity: Jesus as the Final Revelation

Christians believe that Jesus Christ is the ultimate revelation of God, fulfilling the prophecies and promises of the Old Testament. The New Testament writings, particularly the Gospels, capture the life and teachings of Jesus, who is viewed as the culmination of God's redemptive plan.

Islam: Muhammad as the Seal of the Prophets

Islam teaches that Muhammad is the last and final prophet, known as the "Seal of the Prophets." While recognizing previous prophets like Moses, Abraham, and Jesus, Islam holds that Muhammad brought the final and complete revelation in the Quran, which supersedes all previous scriptures.

Concept of Sin and Human Nature

Christianity: Original Sin

Christian doctrine holds that humanity inherits original sin from Adam and Eve's disobedience in the Garden of Eden. This inherent sinful nature necessitates redemption, which Christians believe is provided through Jesus Christ. His death and resurrection offer forgiveness and new life to believers.

Islam: Innate Purity and Accountability

Islam does not embrace the concept of original sin. Instead, it teaches that humans are born in a state of purity and are accountable for their actions. Sin is seen as an act of disobedience to Allah, and individuals are responsible for seeking forgiveness and striving to live righteously.

Religious Practices

Christianity: Sacraments and Worship

Christian worship includes practices such as prayer, singing hymns, reading scripture, and preaching. Sacraments like baptism and the Eucharist (Holy Communion) are vital in many Christian traditions. These sacraments are seen as outward signs of inward grace, instituted by Christ.

Islam: The Five Pillars

Islamic practice is structured around the Five Pillars, which are essential acts of worship and devotion. Salah, the ritual prayer performed five times a day, and Sawm, fasting during the month of Ramadan, are particularly significant. These practices are seen as expressions of faith and obedience to Allah.

Role of Religious Leaders

Christianity: Diverse Clerical Roles

Christianity has a variety of clerical roles depending on the denomination. These include priests, pastors, bishops, and deacons, who lead worship, administer sacraments, and provide spiritual guidance. The Pope, as the bishop of Rome, holds a unique position in the Roman Catholic Church.

Islam: Imams and Scholars

In Islam, religious leadership is provided by imams, who lead prayers and deliver sermons in mosques. Islamic scholars (Ulama) and jurists (Faqih) interpret Sharia law and provide theological guidance. There is no central authoritative figure in Islam akin to the Pope in Christianity.

Eschatology

Christianity: Second Coming and Judgment

Christian eschatology focuses on the second coming of Christ, the resurrection of the dead, and the final judgment. Believers anticipate eternal life with God, while those who reject Christ face eternal separation from God. The Book of Revelation details apocalyptic visions and the ultimate victory of God over evil.

Islam: Day of Judgment

Islamic eschatology emphasizes the Day of Judgment, when all individuals will be resurrected and judged by Allah. Believers who have lived righteously and followed Islamic teachings are rewarded with paradise, while non-believers and sinners face punishment in hell. The Mahdi and the return of Jesus are also significant elements in Islamic end-times beliefs.

View on Other Religions

Christianity: Exclusivity of Christ

Christianity teaches that Jesus is the only way to God (John 14:6). This exclusivist view means that salvation is available only through faith in Jesus Christ. While there are varying perspectives within Christianity about the fate of non-Christians, the central claim remains that Jesus is the unique and final revelation of God.

Islam: Inclusivity with Supremacy

Islam recognizes the legitimacy of previous Abrahamic faiths (Judaism and Christianity) to a certain extent, referring to Jews and Christians as "People of the Book." However, Islam asserts that it is the final and complete way of life, and the Quran is the ultimate revelation that supersedes previous scriptures. Conversion to Islam is encouraged, and it is viewed as the true faith that completes the teachings of earlier prophets.

Conclusion

The theological differences between Christianity and Islam are profound and multifaceted, encompassing their views on God, Jesus Christ, scriptures, salvation, prophets, sin, religious practices, leadership, eschatology, and attitudes towards other religions. Understanding these differences is crucial for interfaith dialogue and for adherents of both faiths to appreciate the distinctiveness of their beliefs and practices. While both religions share a common heritage in their Abrahamic roots, their theological trajectories have led them down divergent paths, each with its own unique claims and traditions.

DR. MAXWELL SHIMBA

CHAPTER 01

IS THE GOD OF ISLAM (ALLAH S.W) THE SAME AS THE GOD OF CHRISTIANS (JEHOVAH)?

For more than twenty years, it has become common to hear lectures by Islamic scholars, spreading across various parts of the world. These scholars teach communities using the Quran and the Bible, claiming that there is only one God. They say that in Hebrew, God is called Jehovah, in Arabic, Allah, in English, God, and in Swahili, Mungu. Therefore, they assert that the God referred to as Allah in the Quran is the same as Jehovah in the Bible. These lectures, often conducted by Muslims, have spread widely. For instance, in Tanzania, there are many groups, one of which is called Al-Marid International Propagation Center. They have written on their banner, quoting from the Bible, the words of Apostle Paul in Ephesians 4:4-6: "One Lord, one faith...one God and Father of all, who is over all."

Thus, you will see that these Islamic scholars teach communities using the Quran and the Bible, claiming that Allah Subhanahu Wa Ta'ala is Jehovah. They spread this teaching through radio, pamphlets, lectures, books, and video and audio cassettes. This has led some Christians to leave their faith and convert to Islam. Some other Christians, though not changing their religion, still believe this. The crucial question for every Christian to ask is, "Is it true that the God Allah as narrated in the Quran is the same as Jehovah as taught in the Bible?" I urge you to follow this lesson carefully to know the truth...

Main Sections of This Lesson:

1. Arguments by Muslims that Allah is Jehovah.

2. Is the name of God in the Quran and the Bible the same?

3. Is the chief angel of Allah the same as Jehovah's?

4. Who is the Creator, Allah or Jehovah?

5. Is the city chosen by Allah the same as Jehovah's?

6. Does Allah's teaching about self-purification match Jehovah's?

7. Is the heaven of Jehovah the same as that of Allah?

8. What is the ultimate fate of those who worship Allah?

1. Arguments by Muslims that Allah is Jehovah

Islamic scholars say that Allah is Jehovah because the prophets of God according to the Bible and the Quran taught that there is only one God. They read these verses...

Prophet Moses said:

Deuteronomy 6:4

"Hear, O Israel: The LORD our God, the LORD is one."

Prophet Isaiah said:

Isaiah 45:18,21

"For this is what the LORD says—he who created the heavens, he is God; he who fashioned and made the earth, he founded it...Is it not I, the LORD? And there is no God apart from me, a righteous God and a Savior; there is none but me."

Prophet David said:

Psalms 86:10

"For you are great and do marvelous deeds; you alone are God."

Jesus said:

John 17:3

"Now this is eternal life: that they know you, the only true God, and Jesus Christ, whom you have sent."

Paul also said:

1 Corinthians 8:4

"So then, about eating food sacrificed to idols: We know that 'An idol is nothing at all in the world' and that 'There is no God but one.'"

Here, Islamic scholars say that all the prophets according to the Bible teach that there is only one God. What did Muhammad (s.a.w.) teach about God? They read these verses from the Quran...

Quran 41:6 (Surah Ha-Mim As-Sajdah)

"Say, 'I am only a human being like you. It is revealed to me that your God is one God.'"

Here, scholars say that just as all the prophets taught one God, so did Muhammad.

Quran 29:46-47 (Surah Al-Ankabut)

"And do not argue with the People of the Book except in the best way possible, unless they transgress, and say, 'We believe in what has been revealed to us and what has been revealed to you. Our God and your God is one, and to Him we submit.' And thus We have revealed to you the Book. Those to whom We gave the Scripture believe in it, and among these are those who believe in it. And none reject Our revelations except the disbelievers."

Here, Islamic scholars after reading these verses, say that the books of the Torah and the Gospel do not contradict the Quran, and that these books were given to the Jews and Christians, and that the God of Muslims and Christians is one.

Is this argument true? I will answer it later.

Answers Regarding One God

When you quickly look at how these Islamic scholars compare verses from the Quran and the Bible, you might be tempted to believe what they teach. But it is good for us to learn in depth according to the Quran and the Bible and then see if there is any truth in their teachings that Allah Subhanahu Wa Ta'ala is Jehovah. Remember that the God we worship warned us Christians by saying...

Exodus 20:1-3

"And God spoke all these words: 'I am the LORD your God, who brought you out of Egypt, out of the land of slavery. You shall have no other gods before me.'"

This warning from our God, saying, "You shall have no other gods," implies that other gods worshipped by people exist. In the Bible, the word for God in Hebrew is "Elohim" and in Greek "Theos," it is mentioned 3,979 times, but also false gods are mentioned 271 times. Some of these false gods are:

- Dagon (Judges 16:23)
- Baal (1 Kings 18:21)
- Artemis, the goddess of the Ephesians (Acts 19:24-28)

Additionally, when we read the Quran, it also mentions various gods worshipped in Mecca, including:

Quran 53:19-20,23 (Surah An-Najm)

"Have you then considered al-Lat and al-Uzza? And another, the third (goddess), Manat? These are but names which you have named, you and your fathers, for which Allah has sent down no authority..."

Thus, we see that many gods are worshipped, and each worshipper depends on their god and says that their god is one. For example, those who worshipped Dagon said he was one god, those who worshipped Baal said he was one god, and those who worshipped Artemis said she was the great god. Similarly, the prophets served one God called Jehovah, while Muhammad worshipped one god called Allah. What I want to teach the community to know is whether Allah is Jehovah.

2. Is the name of God according to the Quran and the Bible the same?

One fundamental thing that identifies something, a person, an animal, or anything else is a name. So, to know if the God worshipped by Muslims is the same one we worship as Christians, we must look at the name. Is it the same?

Quran 17:110 (Surah Bani Isra'il)

"Say, 'Call upon Allah or call upon the Most Merciful. Whichever [name] you call - to Him belong the best names...'"

Here we see Allah teaching Muslims to call upon Him by the name Allah or the Most Merciful. When you read the Quran, you see the name Allah mentioned 2,866 times. Remember, the Quran has 30 parts (Juz), 114 Surahs. Therefore, the God worshipped by Muslims according to the Quran is named Allah.

The name of the God worshipped by Christians is:

Exodus 6:2-3

"God also said to Moses, 'I am the LORD. I appeared to Abraham, to Isaac and to Jacob as God Almighty, but by my name the LORD (Jehovah) I did not make myself fully known to them.'"

Here we see the God we worship as Christians identifying His name as Jehovah. In the Bible, the word or name LORD is used. In English, it is said LORD, meaning the holy name of God. In the Bible, this name is mentioned 6,751 times. Remember, the Bible has a total of 66 books, 1,189 chapters, and 31,102 verses.

3. Is the chief angel of Allah the same as Jehovah's?

If Allah is Jehovah, then clearly, the chief angel would be the same too. If they are not the same, then the chief angels would also be different. Let's start by looking at what Allah narrates in the Quran, saying...

Quran 81:19-21 (Surah At-Takwir)

"Indeed, it is a noble Messenger who has brought it down, [who is] possessed of power and with the Owner of the Throne, secure [in position], obeyed there [in the heavens] and trustworthy."

The explanation within the Quran of these verses (81:19-21) teaches this...

The noble and obedient messenger in heaven is Gabriel, who is the chief of all angels.

The chief angel of Jehovah is:

Jude 1:9

"But even the archangel Michael, when he was disputing with the devil about the body of Moses, did not himself dare to condemn him for slander but said, 'The Lord rebuke you!'"

Here we see the verses teaching us clearly that the chief angel of Allah is called Gabriel, while the chief angel of our God Jehovah is called Michael. Question: Since these angels are different, is Allah Jehovah?

To know more about the differences between the angels, get a copy of the lesson: "Is Gabriel the same as Jibril?" We have that lesson, get it.

4. Who is the Creator, Allah or Jehovah?

Everyone who follows a religion believes that God is the Creator who created human beings, animals, and everything we see and do not see. Thus, it is appropriate to look at what Jehovah says about creation and what Allah says. Do their statements agree or differ?

In whose image is man created?

Allah says:

Quran 112:1-4 (Surah Al-Ikhlas)

"Say, 'He is Allah, [who is] One, Allah, the Eternal Refuge. He neither begets nor is born, Nor is there to Him any equivalent.'"

According to this verse, Allah says that God neither begets nor is born, nor does He have any equivalent. Jehovah says this about man or people...

Genesis 1:26-27

"Then God said, 'Let us make mankind in our image, in our likeness, so that they may rule over the fish in the sea and the birds in the sky, over the livestock and all the wild animals, and over all the creatures that move along the ground.' So God created mankind in his own image, in the image of God he created them; male and female he created them."

Here we see that our God Jehovah created man in His own image, but Allah says He has no equivalent. Question for you, the reader: Is Allah Jehovah? Please read these verses to know more (Genesis 5:1-2, 9:6, 1 Corinthians 11:7, Colossians 1:15, 3:10, Acts 17:28-29, James 3:9). You might ask, "How does God resemble me?" Know that God is Spirit (John 4:24), and He gave us breath (that is, the spirit of life) (Genesis 2:7). Moreover, God is the Father of our spirits (Hebrews 12:9), and He says our spirits belong to Him (Ezekiel 18:4, Numbers 16:22).

Swearing by God about Creation

Quran 91:1-7 (Surah Ash-Shams)

"By the sun and its brightness, and the moon when it follows it, and the day when it displays it, and the night when it covers it, and the sky and He who constructed it, and the earth and He who spread it, and the soul and He who proportioned it."

Quran 92:1-3 (Surah Al-Layl)

"By the night when it covers, and the day when it appears, and [by] He who created the male and female."

Here we see Allah, the God worshipped by Muslims, swearing by the sky and by the One who built it, by the earth and by the One who spread it. Who is this spreader of the earth and builder of the sky? The Quran continues to narrate...

Quran 45:22 (Surah Al-Jathiyah)

"And Allah created the heavens and the earth in truth..."

Quran 44:7-8 (Surah Ad-Dukhan)

"The Lord of the heavens and the earth and whatever is between them, if you would be certain. There is no deity except Him; He gives life and causes death. [He is] your Lord and the Lord of your first forefathers."

Here we see that Allah, through the Quran, says that Allah created the heavens and the earth and that there is no deity except Him. The builder of the sky and spreader of the earth introduces Himself...

Isaiah 44:24

"This is what the LORD says—your Redeemer, who formed you in the womb: 'I am the LORD, the Maker of all things, who stretches out the heavens, who spreads out the earth by myself.'"

Our God Jehovah says, "I make all things."

(Read Isaiah 45:6-7, 11-12, Jeremiah 27:5) Without a doubt, Jehovah is the creator of all things.

Did Jehovah swear by His creation like Allah?

Isaiah 45:22-23

"Turn to me and be saved, all you ends of the earth; for I am God, and there is no other. By myself, I have sworn; my mouth has uttered in all integrity a word that will not be revoked: Before me, every knee will bow; by me, every tongue will swear."

Hebrews 6:13-16

"When God made his promise to Abraham, since there was no one greater for him to swear by, he swore by himself, saying, 'I will surely bless you and give you many descendants.' And so after waiting patiently, Abraham received what was promised. People swear by someone greater than themselves, and the oath confirms what is said and puts an end to all argument."

Here we see that our God Jehovah does not swear by anyone or anything He created like Allah swears. Instead, Jehovah says, "I swear by myself." You can also read how Jehovah swore by Himself in these verses (Isaiah 14:24 and Genesis 22:16).

5. Is the city chosen by Allah the same as Jehovah's?

The City of Allah:

Quran 27:91 (Surah An-Naml)

"I have been commanded to worship the Lord of this city (Makkah), who made it sacred and to whom belongs all things."

Quran 3:96 (Surah Aal-Imran)

"Indeed, the first House [of worship] established for mankind was that at Makkah - blessed and a guidance for the worlds."

Quran 106:3-4 (Surah Quraysh)

"Let them worship the Lord of this House, who has fed them, [saving them] from hunger and made them safe, [saving them] from fear."

Thus, we see that Allah is the Lord of Al-Ka'ba according to these verses, and Al-Ka'ba is in Makkah. These verses show that the God worshipped by Muslims, Allah has chosen Makkah as His holy city, and Muhammad was commanded to worship the Lord of that city, Makkah, who is Allah.

The City Chosen by Our God Jehovah:

2 Chronicles 6:4-6

"And he said: 'Praise be to the LORD, the God of Israel, who with his hands has fulfilled what he promised with his mouth to my father David. For he said, "Since the day I brought my people out of Egypt, I have not chosen a city in any tribe of Israel to have a temple built so that my Name might be there, nor have I chosen anyone to be ruler over my people Israel. But now I have chosen Jerusalem for my Name to be there, and I have chosen David to rule my people Israel."'"

These scriptures do not mention any other city chosen by our God here on earth but only the city of Jerusalem. (see 2 Chronicles 12:13, Ezra 6:12; 7:15,27; Psalms 26:8; Zechariah 2:12)

Through these verses, we see that our God Jehovah has chosen Jerusalem as His city. The word "Jerusalem" is in Hebrew, and it means "foundation of peace." Even when the Israelites were far from the city of Jerusalem, they knelt and faced Jerusalem (see Daniel 6:10). The city chosen by Jehovah is Jerusalem, and the city chosen by Allah is Makkah. This is the difference between the city of Allah and Jehovah.

6. Does Allah's teaching about self-purification match Jehovah's?

Allah's Teaching:

Quran 53:32 (Surah An-Najm)

"Those who avoid the major sins and immoralities, only [committing] slight ones. Indeed, your Lord is vast in forgiveness. He was most knowing of you when He created you from the earth and when you were fetuses in your mothers' wombs. So do not claim yourselves to be pure; He is most knowing of who fears Him."

Quran 12:53 (Surah Yusuf)

"And I do not acquit myself. Indeed, the soul is a persistent enjoiner of evil, except those upon which my Lord has mercy. Indeed, my Lord is Forgiving and Merciful."

According to the Quran, Allah has a soul too (see Quran 5:116). So here we see Allah instructing people not to purify their souls and even saying, "I do not purify my soul." This is very surprising!

Jehovah's Teaching on Self-Purification (Holiness):

Isaiah 43:3

"For I am the LORD your God, the Holy One of Israel, your Savior; I give Egypt for your ransom, Cush and Seba in your stead."

Here we see God saying, "I am holy," which is also a descriptive name of our God Jehovah. In Hebrew, it is said as "kadosh." Prophet Isaiah has written that God is holy 32 times. Just read Isaiah 40:25, 48:17, and 57:15. Moreover, since our God Jehovah is holy, He also commanded us as follows:

Leviticus 11:44

"I am the LORD your God; consecrate yourselves and be holy because I am holy. Do not make yourselves unclean by any creature that moves along the ground."

Apostle Peter instructs us:

1 Peter 1:15-16

"But just as he who called you is holy, so be holy in all you do; for it is written: 'Be holy because I am holy.'"

Apostle Paul also instructed self-purification and holiness (2 Corinthians 7:1). You can also read this instruction to be holy in Leviticus 19:2, 20:26.

Thus, we see Jehovah instructing us to purify our souls to be holy, but Allah instructs Muslims not to purify their souls.

Question for you, the reader, Is Allah Jehovah?

7. Is the heaven of Jehovah the same as the heaven of Allah?

Jehovah's Heaven:

Luke 20:34-36

"Jesus replied, 'The people of this age marry and are given in marriage. But those who are considered worthy of taking part in the age to come and in the resurrection from the dead will neither marry nor be given in marriage, and they can no longer die; for they are like the angels. They are God's children, since they are children of the resurrection.'"

These scriptures confirm to Christians that when we are resurrected and enter heaven, there will be no marriages, as we will have spiritual bodies (1 Corinthians 15:43-54). Additionally, scriptures teach that the kingdom of God is not about eating and drinking but righteousness, peace, and joy in the Holy Spirit (Romans 14:17). Our God clearly teaches that in heaven, there is no hunger, thirst, or sun to harm us (Revelation 7:16-17).

The Heaven of Allah:

1. Mansions

Quran 39:20 (Surah Az-Zumar)

"But those who fear their Lord will have lofty mansions, built one above the other, beneath which rivers flow. This is the promise of Allah; Allah does not fail in His promise."

2. Rivers of Water, Milk, Wine, Honey, and Fruits

Quran 47:15 (Surah Muhammad)

"The description of Paradise, which the righteous are promised, is that in it are rivers of water incorruptible; rivers of milk of which the taste never changes; rivers of wine, a joy to those who drink; and rivers of honey pure and clear. In it there are for them all kinds of fruits and forgiveness from their Lord..."

3. Women with Beautiful Eyes and Meat of Birds

Quran 56:15-23 (Surah Al-Waqi'ah)

"And [there will be] meat of birds, from whatever they desire. And [for them are] fair women with large, [beautiful] eyes, the likenesses of pearls well-protected."

Quran 37:48-49 (Surah As-Saffat)

"And with them will be women limiting [their] glances, with large, [beautiful] eyes, As if they were [delicate] eggs, well protected."

Quran 37:44-46 (Surah As-Saffat)

"On thrones facing one another. There will be circulated among them a cup [of wine] from a flowing spring, White and delicious to the drinkers."

From these verses, we see that Allah Subhanahu Wa Ta'ala, the God worshipped by Muslims, has promised to admit Muslims to heaven, where they will have rivers of water, milk, wine, and honey. They will also have fruits, meat of birds, and be married to women with beautiful eyes.

The most surprising thing is when we read the book of Hadith, because the Islamic religion is also built on the books of Hadith. Read:

Quran 42:10 (Surah Ash-Shura)

"And in anything over which you disagree - its ruling is [to be referred] to Allah. [Say], 'That is Allah, my Lord; upon Him I have relied, and to Him I turn back.'"

When we read the book of Hadith of the Prophet titled Sunan Ibn Majah vol. 5 page 546 Hadith No: 4337, it states:

"Abu 'Umamah reported that the Messenger of Allah (peace and blessings of Allah be upon him) said Allah will marry him to seventy-two wives; two will be from the virgins with big eyes and seventy will be his inheritance from the people of Hell. Everyone will have a pleasant vagina, and the man will have a sexual organ that does not bend down (during intercourse)."

In English, this Hadith reads:

"Abu Umamah reported that Allah's messenger said Allah will not admit anyone in the paradise but Allah, the mighty and glorious, will marry him with seventy-two wives; two will be from the virgins with big eyes and seventy will be his inheritance from the people of Hell. Everyone of them will have a pleasant vagina, and he will have a sexual organ that does not bend down (during sexual intercourse)."

This is what Allah, the God of Muslims, has promised. This is something that greatly surprises Christians because what Allah teaches is not found at all with our God Jehovah. Here on earth is where we have intoxication, fruits, meat, marriages, mansions, cars, rivers, seas, and other things.

Think about it, who is this Allah?

8. What is the ultimate fate of those who worship Allah?

We know that Christians will live with our God Jehovah forever (see 1 Thessalonians 4:13-17 and Revelation 21:3-7). Our God is eternal. However, when we read the Quran and the Hadiths of Muhammad, the prophet of Muslims, we see these teachings...

Quran 51:56 (Surah Adh-Dhariyat)

"I did not create the jinn and mankind except to worship Me."

Quran 6:128 (Surah Al-An'am)

"And [mention, O Muhammad], the Day when He will gather them together [and say], 'O company of jinn, you have misled many of mankind.' And their allies among mankind will say, 'Our Lord, some of us made use of others, and we have [now] reached our term which You appointed for us.' He will say, 'The Fire is your residence, wherein you will abide eternally, except for what Allah wills. Indeed, your Lord is Wise and Knowing.'"

In these verses, we see that jinn and all people will be thrown into hell. What about Allah? When we read the book of Hadith of the Prophet (s.a.w.) titled Sahih al-Bukhari Vol. VI Hadith No: 371, page 353, it states:

Quran 50:30 (Surah Qaf)

"The Day We will say to Hell, 'Are you filled?' And it will say, 'Are there any more?'"

Narrated Anas: The Prophet said people will be thrown into the (Hell) Fire and it will say, "Are there any more (to come)?" till Allah puts His Foot over it and it will say, "Qat! Qat!" (Enough! Enough!).

In English, this Hadith reads:

"Allah's statement: 'It (Hell) will say: Are there any more (to come)?' (50:30). Narrated Anas: The Prophet said the people will be thrown into the (Hell) Fire and it will say: 'Are there any more (to come)?' till Allah puts His Foot over it and it will say: 'Qat! Qat!' (Enough! Enough!)."

In this verse, we see Allah, the God of Muslims, asking Hell if it is full, and Hell will ask Allah if there is more. This question indicates that Hell was not yet full.

The description of this Hadith confirms that Allah will put His foot in Hell, and then Hell will say, "Enough! Enough!" meaning it will be full by the act of Allah putting His foot in it. This is very different from our God Jehovah. Our God has made hell specifically for evil people, the devil, and his angels. Please read these verses: Matthew 25:41,46; Revelation 20:10, 21:8.

All these verses show that the end of the wicked, the devil, and his angels is in the lake of fire. Dear reader, who is this Allah?

I hope you have been able to understand deeply through the Quran, the Bible, and the Hadith books of the Prophet of Muslims named Muhammad that Allah Subhanahu Wa Ta'ala, the God worshipped by Muslims, is not Jehovah, the God we worship as Christians.

CHAPTER 02

WHERE DID ALLAH COME FROM?

Islam claims that Allah is the same God who engaged with the Jews since the times of Abraham in the Old Testament. But is this true?

Islam began with Muhammad around 600 AD. What were the beliefs of the Arabs before him? Are there any elements from these beliefs that made their way into Islam? In other words, does Islam have any pagan influences?

Join me in this comprehensive article that examines the origins of Islam to see if there is any relationship between Islam and the paganism that was prevalent among the Arab societies before Muhammad's arrival.

The Origin of Allah

Human societies worldwide have always wondered about the origin of the world, the meaning of life, and where people go after death. As a result, each society came to believe in a powerful entity (or entities) greater than humans, who deserved worship and were called upon for help during times of trouble.

These powerful beings were known by various names in different societies. Similarly, each society established specific rituals for communicating with these deities.

One thing is clear: EXCEPT FOR THE JEWISH COMMUNITY, all other human societies worldwide—whether in Africa, Europe, Asia, etc.—started with pagan worship. These societies worshipped various gods. These gods were represented by things like mountains, large trees, the sun, the moon, giant serpents, statues, kings, etc. For instance, the Romans had gods like Artemis, Jupiter, Minerva, Atlas, etc. The Greeks had gods like Chronos, Dionysus, Eros, Ares, Apollo, Hermes, Poseidon, etc. The Indians have gods like Durga, Ganesha, Garuda, Brahma, etc. These pagan beliefs even grew and spread widely. For instance, Buddhism is a pagan belief that spread across a large part of Asia—India, Japan, Sri Lanka, China, etc.

Therefore, the Arab societies, like other human societies, also had their pagan worship practices.

The Arabs worshipped what is known today as the "star family." It is called the 'star family' because they attributed human characteristics to their gods. The moon was considered a male god and the sun his wife. Together they had children. For instance, they believed they had three daughters known as Al-Lat, Al-Uzza, and Manat.

That's why even the Quran mentions: "Have you considered Al-Lat and Al-Uzza, and another, the third (goddess) Manat?" (Surah 53:19-20).

Meaning: Have you seen Al-Lat and Al-Uzza, and the other, the third (goddess) Manat?

Even Muhammad worshipped these gods before founding Islam. We read from Hisham al-Kalbi's "Kitab al-Asnam" (Book of Idols), page 17:

'We have been told that the Apostle of Allah once mentioned al-Uzza saying, "I have offered a white sheep to al-'Uzza, while I was a follower of the religion of my people."'

Meaning: We were told that the Messenger of Allah once mentioned al-Uzza saying, "I offered a white sheep to al-Uzza while I was following the religion of my people." His people were the Quraysh.

The name Allah comes from al-ilah. Al is like the English article 'a'; and ilah means god. So, al ilah means 'a god' or simply 'god' in Swahili—because Swahili lacks an equivalent of 'a.'

As languages evolve, this name was shortened to 'Allah.' It's similar to how in Swahili, someone might say 'mambo ndo ivo bwana.' Actually, 'ndo ivo' is short for 'ndiyo hivyo.' Maybe fifty or a hundred years from now, people won't know that the origin of 'ndo ivo' is the words 'ndiyo hivyo.'

So, who was Allah? Allah was the moon god, whose wife was the sun, and their children (daughters) were Al-Lat, Al-Uzza, and Manat. These were considered the chief gods among the many gods worshipped by the Arabs before Islam—a period Muslims call 'Jahiliyah' (ignorance).

This name 'Allah' is masculine; hence one of his daughters was named 'Al-Lat,' which is feminine. It's like how Francis and Fortunatus are male names, but Francisca and Fortunata are female names—even though the names have the same root. The same applies to Allah and Al-Lat. It's the same name, differing only in gender.

One of the tribes that worshipped Allah extensively was the Quraysh tribe, from which Muhammad originated.

People who don't understand think that Allah became known after Muhammad's emergence. Others claim that Allah was known since the time of Abraham as He is known today. If that were true, they need to ask how the Allah of Abraham disappeared and became a pagan Allah.

For instance, it's well-known that Muhammad's father was not a Muslim but a pagan.

I wouldn't be surprised if some Muslims claimed that Muhammad's father was a Muslim. However, this man died before Muhammad was even born. What does Muhammad himself say about his father?

We read this:

Anas reported: Verily, a person said: Messenger of Allah, where is my father? He said: (He) is in the Fire. When he turned away, he (the Holy Prophet) called him and said: Verily, my father and your father are in the Fire. (Sahih Muslim, Book 001, Number 0398).

Meaning: Anas reported: Truly, a person said: Messenger of Allah, where is my father? He said: He is in the Fire. When he turned away, the Holy Prophet called him and said: Truly, my father and your father are in the Fire.

And the question we would like them to ask themselves is, why was Muhammad's pagan father called 'Abdullah'?

Since 'Abdullah' means 'servant of Allah,' this is a clear sign that the pagans of the Jahiliyah period worshipped Allah to the extent of naming their children in honor of Allah—just as the Jews named their children in honor of the God of Abraham, Isaac, and Jacob.

For example:

- Joshua – Yahweh is salvation;

- Jotham – Yahweh is perfect;

- Jehoahaz – Yahweh has seized;

- Hezekiah – Yahweh has strengthened;

- Elisha – God is salvation, etc.

The answer is clear. Allah was a pagan god worshipped before Islam came. This god was the 'moon god,' also known as 'al-ilah.' Another name for him was 'Hubal.' This pagan god was worshipped throughout the Middle East, not just by the Arabs.

This fact has been repeatedly confirmed by archaeologists—who excavate ancient artifacts—who have uncovered many items showing how moon, sun, and star worship was prevalent throughout the Middle East.

And that's why Muhammad's father, Abdullah, was almost sacrificed by Muhammad's grandfather, Abdul Muttalib. Abdul Muttalib wanted to sacrifice his son as an offering to Allah. But Abdullah's uncle saved him, and instead, 100 camels were sacrificed in his place. And it should be noted that these sacrifices took place at the Kaaba (which we will examine later).

We are told that:

An arrow showed that it was 'Abdullah to be sacrificed. 'Abdul-Muttalib then took the boy to Al-Ka'bah with a razor to slaughter the boy. Quraish, his uncles from Makhzum tribe and his brother Abu Talib, however, tried to dissuade him. They suggested that he summon a she-diviner. She ordered that the divination arrows should be drawn with respect to 'Abdullah as well as ten camels. … the number of the camels (finally) amounted to one hundred. (Ibn Hisham 1/151-155; Rahmat-ul-lil'alameen 2/89, 90).

Meaning: An arrow showed that Abdullah was to be sacrificed. Abdul Muttalib then took the boy to the Kaaba with a razor to slaughter the boy. The Quraysh, his uncles from the Makhzum tribe, and his brother Abu Talib, however, tried to dissuade him. They suggested that he summon a she-diviner. She ordered the divination arrows to be drawn concerning Abdullah and ten camels. … the number of camels finally amounted to one hundred.

That is why the God of the Bible repeatedly warned the Israelites against the pagan practices of the societies around them concerning the worship of the star family or the heavenly host. For example, He says:

"… lest you lift your eyes to heaven, and when you see the sun, the moon, and the stars, all the host of heaven, you feel driven to worship them and serve them, which the Lord your God has given to all the peoples under the whole heaven as a heritage." (Deuteronomy 4:19).

"If there is found among you, within any of your gates which the Lord your God gives you, a man or a woman who has been wicked in the sight of the Lord your God, in transgressing His covenant, who has gone and served other gods and worshiped them, either the sun or moon or any of the host of heaven, which I have not commanded." (Deuteronomy 17:2-3).

"For he rebuilt the high places which Hezekiah his father had destroyed; he raised up altars for Baal, and made a wooden image, as Ahab king of Israel had done; and he worshiped all the host of heaven and served them." (2 Kings 21:3).

"And he built altars for all the host of heaven in the two courts of the house of the Lord." (2 Kings 21:5).

"And he removed the idolatrous priests whom the kings of Judah had ordained to burn incense on the high places in the cities of Judah and in the places all around Jerusalem, and those who burned incense to Baal, to the sun, to the moon, to the constellations, and to all the host of heaven." (2 Kings 23:5).

"They shall spread them before the sun and the moon and all the host of heaven, which they have loved and which they have served, and after which they have walked, which they have sought, and which they have worshiped. They shall not be gathered nor buried; they shall be like refuse on the face of the earth." (Jeremiah 8:2).

"And the houses of Jerusalem and the houses of the kings of Judah shall be defiled like the place of Tophet, because of all the houses on whose roofs they have burned incense to all the host of heaven, and poured out drink offerings to other gods." (Jeremiah 19:13).

"Those who worship the host of heaven on the housetops; those who worship and swear oaths by the Lord, but who also swear by Milcom." (Zephaniah 1:5).

....

In 570 AD, the same year Muhammad was born, there was a ruler of the Aksumite Empire of Ethiopia who resided in Yemen. His name was Abrahah al-Ashram. It is said that he was envious of Mecca for attracting many pilgrims (a pagan pilgrimage), so he built a large church in Sana'a, Yemen, hoping to attract many people, which did not happen.

As a result, he decided to attack Mecca to destroy the Kaaba. He traveled with his many people on a large group of elephants—hence the year became known as the Year of the Elephant.

The Quraysh tribes united to try to save the Kaaba. Abdul Muttalib (Muhammad's grandfather) told the people to hide in the mountains while he and some others stayed near the Kaaba.

But due to the size and strength of Abrahah's army, Abdul Muttalib said:

"The Owner of this House is its Defender, and I am sure He will save it from the attack of the adversaries and will not dishonor the servants of His House."

Meaning: "The Owner of this House is its Defender, and I am sure He will save it from the attack of the adversaries and will not dishonor the servants of His House."

Traditions say that as Abrahah advanced toward the Kaaba, a large flock of birds appeared and started pelting him with stones like rain, wounding him. Thus, his plan to destroy the Kaaba failed, and he returned home injured.

Now, the question is, if at that time Muhammad was still an infant, and thus Islam had not yet begun; and it is known that there were hundreds of pagan gods at the Kaaba; who was the Owner of the House referred to by Abdul Muttalib?

It is clear that this was a pagan god, namely the moon god, Allah, who was worshipped and served by Abdul Muttalib.

The bigger question is, the Quran says in Surah Al-Fil (The Elephant) 105:1-5:

"Have you not seen how your Lord dealt with the owners of the Elephant? Did He not make their treacherous plan go astray? And He sent against them birds in flocks, striking them with stones of baked clay, so He rendered them like straw eaten up."

Meaning:

"Have you not seen how your Lord dealt with the owners of the Elephant? Did He not make their treacherous plan go astray? And He sent against them birds in flocks, striking them with stones of baked clay, so He rendered them like straw eaten up."

The question is, these events occurred during the time of paganism, not Islam. The servant of the pagan god Abdul Muttalib said that the Owner of the House (Kaaba) would defend it.

So, who was the Owner of the House mentioned by Abdul Muttalib, and who is the Lord mentioned in this Surah of the Quran? Or should we say that there were two gods who collaborated to stone Abrahah and his elephants?

Abdul Muttalib did not know the Allah of Muhammad, so he would not have mentioned him (if indeed the Allah of Muhammad is different from that of Abdul Muttalib).

All evidence points to the fact that the moon god, worshipped by Abdul Muttalib, is the one who protected the Kaaba against Abrahah's elephants. Therefore, this verse in the Quran cannot claim to be referring to a different god!

Conclusion

If you are a Muslim, do you not wonder why the moon has so much significance in important matters for Muslims?

Why must the moon be seen for fasting to begin?

Why must the moon be seen for fasting to end?

Why is the main symbol on every mosque a crescent moon and star? What is the origin of these things?

The Kaaba

In part 1 of this article, we examined the origin of Allah. In this second part, we will discuss the city of Mecca and the Kaaba, which is the main shrine of Islam.

Mecca is the center of Islam in the world. It is in this city that the Kaaba, or as Muslims believe and call it, Bait-ul-Haram or Bait-ul-Allah, meaning 'the house of Allah' or 'the house of God,' is located. Every Muslim worldwide is required to pray five times a day facing Mecca, where this house of their God is. Additionally, each one of them is required to go to Mecca for pilgrimage at least once in their lifetime, as pilgrimage is one of the main pillars of Islam. In other words, the Kaaba is the principal shrine in Islam.

The Kaaba is a cuboid structure that, among other things, contains a black stone embedded in one of its corners. Thus, when Muslims go to Mecca for pilgrimage, they circumambulate the Kaaba and either kiss or touch the stone, and if that is not possible, they at least point towards it.

In the past, Allah says that Muhammad used to look up to the heavens when he prayed [I believe everyone who believes in God believes that God is above – and to be honest, that seems to be the most accurate perspective]. But Allah told his prophet:

"We have certainly seen the turning of your face, [O Muhammad], toward the heaven, and We will surely turn you to a qiblah with which you will be pleased. So turn your face toward al-Masjid al-Haram. And wherever you [believers] are, turn your faces toward it [in prayer]. Indeed, those who have been given the Scripture well know that it is the truth from their Lord. And Allah is not unaware of what they do." (Surah Al-Baqarah 2:144) – Sahih International Version.

Meaning:

"We have certainly seen the turning of your face, [O Muhammad], toward the heaven, and We will surely turn you to a qiblah with which you will be pleased. So turn your face toward al-Masjid al-Haram. And wherever you [believers] are, turn your faces toward it [in prayer]. Indeed, those who have been given the Scripture well know that it is the truth from their Lord. And Allah is not unaware of what they do."

Allah says He is not pleased with Muhammad and the Muslims turning their faces up to the heavens (where the Creator of all is – a very strange and puzzling thing!), instead, He commanded them to turn their faces towards the Kaaba wherever they are when they pray.

He also says that those who have been given the Scriptures (i.e., the people of the book) know full well that this is the truth from their Lord!

Oh Allah! Whose Lord is this while you claim to be the one who told Abraham to go and build the Kaaba from Canaan – more than 1,000 kilometers from Mecca? [Moreover, Mecca, which didn't even exist until around 400 AD – so I don't know if Abraham went to build the Kaaba in a wilderness with no people at all]!! Does it mean there is their Lord who is not you then! Then that Lord has his own Abraham and Ishmael; and you have your own Abraham and Ishmael, or what?

According to the Quran, the Kaaba was built by Abraham and his son, Ishmael. The Quran says:

"Remember We made the House a place of assembly for men and a place of safety; and take ye the station of Abraham as a place of prayer; and We covenanted with Abraham and Isma'il, that they should sanctify My House for those who compass it round, or use it as a retreat, or bow, or prostrate themselves (therein in prayer)." [Quran 2:125].

Meaning:

"Remember, We made the House a place of assembly for men and a place of safety; so take the station of Abraham as a place of prayer; and We covenanted with Abraham and Ishmael, that they should sanctify My House for those who compass it round, or use it as a retreat, or bow, or prostrate themselves (therein in prayer)."

[Allah says He made this house for humanity, but Muslims do not allow non-Muslims, especially Christians, to go to the Kaaba; or even fly over it!! It might be that when Allah says 'humanity,' He means 'Muslims'!]

Regarding Abraham, we leave that matter to the Muslims because we believe, that historical and scriptural evidence clearly shows that Abraham never set foot in Arabia.

For example, the following is one piece of evidence on this matter. We read that:

Narrated Abu Dhaar: I said, "O Allah's Apostle! Which mosque was built first?" He replied, "Al-Masjid-ul-Haram." I asked, "Which (was built) next?" He replied, "Al-Masjid-ul-Aqsa." I asked, "What was the period in between them?" He replied, "Forty years." (Sahih Bukhari 4:55:636).

Meaning:

Narrated Abu Dhaar: I said, "O Allah's Apostle! Which mosque was built first?" He replied, "Al-Masjid-ul-Haram." I asked, "Which (was built) next?" He replied, "Al-Masjid-ul-Aqsa." I asked, "What was the period in between them?" He replied, "Forty years."

Muhammad has things! Al-Masjid-ul-Aqsa is the Kaaba. And Al-Masjid-ul-Haram is Solomon's temple in Judaism.

Now, the temple of Jerusalem was built by King Solomon around 950 BC (Before Christ). This means that if Muhammad's words are true – and I believe no Muslim would admit that Muhammad is a liar – then, the mosque at the Kaaba should have been built around 990 BC (adding that 40-year difference).

That is not a problem. But the issue arises when you involve Abraham. Abraham lived around 2000 BC. Look here. This means he lived about 1050 years before the temple of Solomon was built. Now, if Muhammad's Abraham who built the Kaaba built it 40 years before Solomon's temple, then it MUST be a different Abraham and a different Ishmael from those in the Bible. Either way, that is the Muslims' issue to solve. It is up to them to be satisfied and prove to themselves that if they want their faith to come from Abraham who spoke to the God of Israel, then that is the situation!

Based on the above fact, we are left with two possibilities: first, if Muhammad is correct about the 40 years, then Allah is the one who made a mistake or lied saying Abraham built the Kaaba. If Allah is correct, then Muhammad is the one who made a mistake or lied that the Kaaba was built 40 years before Solomon's temple. [However, there is a possibility that this is a completely different Abraham. Let's consider the following:

Even if the Kaaba was built by Abraham (of the Bible or a different one), one thing is clear; by the time Muhammad came and founded his religion, the Kaaba was under the control of the Arabian pagans with more than three hundred gods inside and around it.

In the year 630 AD, Muhammad and his followers took control of the city of Mecca and made the Kaaba a place for worshipping one God instead of more than three hundred gods. [but don't forget, in part 1 of this article, we established that Allah was a pagan god for thousands of years before Muhammad came. And you wonder; what is the origin of 'Allah Akbar,' meaning 'Allah is great'? Isn't it because there were hundreds of gods, including Allah, which is why Muhammad was essentially saying, "No. All these gods are nothing. Allah is greater than all of them"? That is the correct context for saying such words, isn't it? That is just a thought that needs your research as a believer in Allah; because I do not believe that Allah is the God of Abraham, Isaac, and Jacob.]

So let's return to the matter of the presence of hundreds of gods at the Kaaba when Muhammad arrived. Here is what we read:

Narrated 'Abdullah bin Masud: The Prophet entered Mecca and (at that time) there were three hundred-and-sixty idols around the Kaaba. He started stabbing the idols with a stick he had in his hand and reciting: "Truth (Islam) has come and Falsehood (disbelief) has vanished." [Sahih Bukhari 3:43:658].

Meaning:

Narrated 'Abdullah bin Masud: The Prophet entered Mecca and (at that time) there were three hundred and sixty idols around the Kaaba. He started stabbing the idols with a stick he had in his hand and reciting: "Truth (Islam) has come and Falsehood (disbelief) has vanished."

My Muslim friends, the Kaaba has no connection with the Supreme God who created the heavens and the earth. It was just a pagan shrine for worshipping the moon, sun, and stars.

Here is what we are told:

Narrated Abu Huraira: "In the year prior to the last Hajj of the Prophet when Allah's Apostle made Abu Bakr the leader of the pilgrims, the latter (Abu Bakr) sent me in the company of a group of people to make a public announcement: 'No pagan is allowed to perform Hajj after this year, and no naked person is allowed to perform Tawaf of the Kaaba.'" (Bukh

ari V2, B26, 689 (V1, B8, No 365).

Meaning:

Narrated Abu Huraira: "In the year prior to the last Hajj of the Prophet when Allah's Apostle made Abu Bakr the leader of the pilgrims, Abu Bakr sent me in the company of a group of people to make a public announcement: 'No pagan is allowed to perform Hajj after this year, and no naked person is allowed to perform Tawaf of the Kaaba.'"

I don't know if you, the reader, can see the meaning of these words. This is what we read here:

1. Muslims and pagans were performing Hajj together at the Kaaba for many years until Abu Bakr was made the leader.

2. During the Hajj, pagans would perform Tawaf (circumambulation of the Kaaba) while naked.

3. Pagans worshipped their pagan gods at the Kaaba while Muslims worshipped Allah.

To understand the weight of this matter, imagine the Temple of Solomon built in Jerusalem for Yahweh. Inside that temple, Jews worship Yahweh, and pagans worship the sun, moon, and stars; and they do it while naked!!!!!!!

Since that scenario is unimaginable and impossible, the only conclusion is that it was Muhammad who intruded into the pagans' shrine, not the other way around!

That is why Muhammad had the courage to consider demolishing the Kaaba. Here is what we read:

Narrated Aswad: Ibn Az-Zubair said to me, "Aisha used to tell you secretly a number of things. What did she tell you about the Ka'ba?" I replied, "She told me that once the Prophet said, 'O 'Aisha! Had not your people been still close to the pre-Islamic period of ignorance (infidelity)! I would have dismantled the Ka'ba and would have made two doors in it; one for entrance and the other for exit." (Sahih Bukhari 1:3:128).

Meaning:

Narrated Aswad: Ibn Az-Zubair said to me, "Aisha used to tell you secretly a number of things. What did she tell you about the Ka'ba?" I replied, "She told me that once the Prophet said, 'O 'Aisha! Had not your people been still close to the pre-Islamic period of ignorance (infidelity)! I would have dismantled the Ka'ba and would have made two doors in it; one for entrance and the other for exit."

Imagine here too; Moses was told by Yahweh to make a tabernacle. He was given detailed instructions on how everything should be, and he was told to do exactly as shown by Yahweh. Then comes a prophet or messenger hundreds of years later saying, "I think this house of Yahweh was incorrectly built with one door. It should have two doors here." Is that even possible?

So, if it is true that Allah told Abraham and Ishmael to build the Kaaba, does it make sense for Muhammad to say he could demolish it and build two doors?? Can a human correct God?

But that is possible only if the house has no connection to God; just as the Kaaba has no connection to the God of heaven.

Today there are many churches and temples in the world, but when we talk about Moses' tabernacle or King Solomon's temple, we are talking about very special places where God Himself personally gave the measurements and chose the location. Similarly, there are many mosques in the world, but when talking about the mosque at the Kaaba, it is supposed to be Allah Himself (claimed to be the God of Abraham) who directly involved in that work. Now, look at the image below and ask yourself if the God of heaven could command His house to be built in a place with such characteristics:

I told you earlier that the Kaaba has a black stone (called Al-hajar Al-aswad) that Muslims kiss or touch as part of their worship there. But we are told this about the stone:

Later, Umar said to the black stone, "I know that you are a stone, that neither helps nor hurts, and if the messenger of god had not kissed you, I would not kiss you." (Sahih Bukhari, volume 2, 667).

Meaning:

Later, Umar said to the black stone, "I know that you are a stone that neither helps nor hurts, and if the messenger of god had not kissed you, I would not kiss you."

That is the state of Islam and Muslims to this day. Almost everything in Islam is contrary to the reality of life; even their hearts reject it, but what can they do since they have already committed to Muhammad? What Umar is essentially saying is, "In my heart, I feel that this business of kissing a stone is utter vanity, but I have no way to stop because the prophet kissed it."

I believe many Muslims think that the Kaaba existing today is the same one that Allah told them was built by Abraham and Ishmael. But the truth is that the Kaaba has been demolished and rebuilt more than ten times. Look here. So, the one existing today is just a recent construction by the Saudi government.

Conclusion

It is true that the Kaaba is the house of Allah, but it is NEVER the house of the God of Abraham, Isaac, and Jacob. Nor has the Abraham of Israel ever gone to Arabia to build the Kaaba. This was an altar for the moon god, the sun, stars, and more than 360 gods worshipped by the pagans of Arabia. The truth is that this was not the only Kaaba. There were many Kaabas where the pagans there worshipped their gods. You have seen for yourself how these pagans used to go to Mecca for pilgrimage at the Kaaba, even while naked. How can you say today that the same place and the same practices are now for worshiping the God who created the heavens and the earth?

That is why Yahweh warned the Israelites, saying: "You shall therefore keep all my statutes and all my judgments, and perform them, ... And you shall not walk in the statutes of the nation which I am casting out before you; for they commit all these things, and therefore I abhor them." (Leviticus 20:22-23). But strangely, Allah says the exact opposite. Essentially, what he says to Muslims is: "Follow the customs of the people who lived in Mecca"!!!

Does the God of heaven need a house here on earth to live in? With all His greatness, would this God reside in a small room that is empty inside?

Jesus Christ is calling you to give you eternal life now. Time is running fast!

In today's world, getting information is not a problem. We have the largest library ever since the creation of the world, containing every piece of information you want on earth - the Internet. It is up to you to know what you want.

CHAPTER 03

IS JIBRIL OF THE QURAN THE SAME AS GABRIEL OF THE BIBLE?

Since the establishment of the Islamic faith, Muslims worldwide have believed and taught that the angel called 'Gabriel' in the Holy Scriptures of the Bible is the same angel 'Jibril' as narrated in the Quran.

The important question is: Is it true that the angel "Gabriel" is "Jibril"? I urge you to follow this lesson to find out the truth….

Muslim Arguments for Believing Gabriel is Jibril

Muslims compare verses from the Quran and the Bible and say that the angel Gabriel is Jibril, citing these verses:

Quran 19:16-17 (Surat Maryam)

16. And mention, [O Muhammad], in the Book [the story of] Mary, when she withdrew from her family to a place toward the east.

17. And she took, in seclusion from them, a screen. Then We sent to her Our Angel, and he represented himself to her as a well-proportioned man.

Luke 1:26-28

26. In the sixth month, the angel Gabriel was sent from God to a city of Galilee named Nazareth,

27. to a virgin betrothed to a man whose name was Joseph, of the house of David. And the virgin's name was Mary.

28. And he came to her and said, "Greetings, O favored one, the Lord is with you!"

Apart from reading these verses, they also refer to the book on the life of Prophet Muhammad written by the late Sheikh Abdallah Saleh Al-Farsy, the former Chief Kadhi of Kenya. On page 17, section (A), it states:

HOW REVELATION WAS BROUGHT

Muslims believe that the Quran is the word of Allah, just as the Torah of Moses, the Gospel of Jesus, and the Psalms of David are also words of Allah. However, Allah is not seen by the naked eye, nor is He in a specific place. So how did these prophets receive these words? The answer is that they received them through Jibril, the greatest of all angels.

Quran 53:2-6 (Surat An-Najm)

2. Your companion [Muhammad] has not strayed, nor has he erred,

3. Nor does he speak from [his own] inclination.

4. It is not but a revelation revealed,

5. Taught to him by one intense in strength

6. One of soundness. And he rose to [his] true form.

Muslims, by reading these verses, believe the angel Gabriel is Jibril, but these verses show differences because the angel Jibril was sent by Allah (who is not Jehovah) to Mary, who was in a mosque, and the Quran does not mention the city or country Jibril went to. However, the Bible teaches that the angel Gabriel entered Mary's house. Additionally, the Bible teaches that the revelation of prophecy was brought by the guidance of the Holy Spirit (2 Peter 1:20-21), not by the angel Jibril as the Quran narrates.

WHAT KIND OF BEINGS ARE ANGELS?

Hebrews 1:13-14

13. To which of the angels did God ever say, "Sit at my right hand until I make your enemies a footstool for your

feet"?14. Are not all angels ministering spirits sent to serve those who will inherit salvation?

It is clear that angels are beings with a spiritual nature and have the ability to appear to people in human form (e.g., Genesis 18:1-19:12), as seen when they appeared to Abraham and Lot. An angel appeared to Moses in the form of a burning bush (Exodus 3:1-5).

ARE ALL ANGELS GOOD AND DO THEY NEVER DISOBEY GOD?

Reading the Quran, we see that Allah, worshipped by Muslims, narrates that angels are beings with these qualities:

Quran 16:93 (Surat An-Nahl)

"And if Allah had willed, He could have made you [of] one religion, but He causes to stray whom He wills and guides whom He wills. And you will surely be questioned about what you used to do."

Quran 32:13 (Surat As-Sajdah)

"And if We had willed, We could have given every soul its guidance, but the word from Me will come into effect [that] 'I will surely fill Hell with jinn and people all together.'"

EXPLANATION OF QURAN 32:13

If Allah had willed, He could have created humans like angels who cannot do evil, and whose nature is only to do good; hence, they are not rewarded for their good because they do it without struggle. But humans were created with the ability to do both good and evil.

According to these verses, Allah, worshipped by Muslims, says that angels are good and cannot do evil; they are one group that all obey Allah. However, referring to the Bible, we see our God Jehovah has revealed to His apostles that angels are like this:

2 Peter 2:4

"For if God did not spare angels when they sinned, but sent them to hell, putting them in chains of darkness to be held for judgment."

These sinful angels are under the devil. Besides the sinful ones, there are also angels like this:

Matthew 25:31

"When the Son of Man comes in his glory, and all the angels with him, he will sit on his glorious throne."

According to these verses, we see clearly that our God teaches there are two groups of angels, the good (holy) and the bad (sinners). Allah does not describe this because he says all angels are good and cannot do evil. This teaches us that Allah is not Jehovah.

MEANING OF THE NAME GABRIEL

The word or name "Gabriel" originates from Hebrew and means "Messenger of God." In the Bible, this name is mentioned four times (see Daniel 8:16 and 9:21, Luke 1:19 and 1:26). The angel Gabriel is often shown as being sent by God to bring good news regarding human salvation and offers comforting words, saying, "Do not be afraid." The Bible mentions the angel Gabriel 366 times. When we read the Bible, we also see this angel referred to as the "Angel of the Lord." This phrase appears 65 times in about 61 verses. If all these references pertain to the angel Gabriel, then he is mentioned many times.

HOW TO KNOW THE DIFFERENCE BETWEEN THE ANGEL GABRIEL AND JIBRIL

1 Timothy 4:1

"The Spirit clearly says that in later times some will abandon the faith and follow deceiving spirits and things taught by demons."

(See also Matthew 7:15-20)

1 John 4:1, 3, 15

1. "Dear friends, do not believe every spirit, but test the spirits to see whether they are from God, because many false prophets have gone out into the world."

3. "but every spirit that does not acknowledge Jesus is not from God. This is the spirit of the antichrist, which you have heard is coming and even now is already in the world."

15. "If anyone acknowledges that Jesus is the Son of God, God lives in them and they in God."

The important thing is to test between Jibril and Gabriel who acknowledges Jesus as the Son of God. If their teachings are the same, then they are not two different angels but one. If they differ, then they are not the same but two completely different angels.

IS THE RANK OF THE ANGEL GABRIEL THE SAME AS JIBRIL?

THE ANGEL GABRIEL SENT BY GOD JEHOVAH SAYS:

Luke 1:19

"The angel answered, 'I am Gabriel. I stand in the presence of God, and I have been sent to speak to you and to tell you this good news.'"

According to this verse, the angel Gabriel explains that he stands in the presence of God, indicating that his rank is as a messenger standing before God. Does the angel Jibril, sent by the god called Allah, hold the same rank as Gabriel?

Quran 81:19-21 (Surat At-Takwir)

19. "Indeed, the Quran is a word [conveyed by] a noble messenger [Jibril],"

20. "Who is possessed of power and with the Owner of the Throne, secure [in position],"

21. "Obeyed there [in the heavens] and trustworthy."

EXPLANATION OF QURAN 81:19-21

The noble messenger obeyed in heaven is "Jibril," who is the chief of all angels.

WHO IS THE CHIEF ANGEL OF JEHOVAH?

Jude 1:9

"But even the archangel Michael, when he was disputing with the devil about the body of Moses, did not himself dare to condemn him for slander but said, 'The Lord rebuke you!'"

In this verse, we see that the chief angel of our God Jehovah, whom Christians worship, is Michael, while the chief angel of Allah, whom Muslims worship, is Jibril. Thus, Jibril is not Gabriel. Referring to the chief angel "Michael," this is a name with Hebrew origin, meaning "Who is like God." He led other angels in fighting against Satan and cast him out of heaven when he exalted himself to be like God (see Revelation 12:7-12 and Daniel 10:13,21; 12:2).

THEIR TEACHINGS ABOUT

THE SON OF GOD

(A) THE ANGEL GABRIEL OF GOD JEHOVAH TAUGHT THIS:

Luke 1:26-35 (quoting verse 35 only)

"The angel answered, 'The Holy Spirit will come on you, and the power of the Most High will overshadow you. So the holy one to be born will be called the Son of God.'"

(B) THE ANGEL JIBRIL OF ALLAH SAYS THIS:

Quran 18:4-5 (Surat Al-Kahf)

4. "And to warn those who say, 'Allah has taken a son.'"

5. "They have no knowledge of it, nor do their forefathers. Grave is the word that comes out of their mouths; they speak not except a lie."

These words taught by the angel Jibril (Quran 53:5-6) blaspheme our God Jehovah (see Exodus 4:22). God says, "Israel is my firstborn son," and His angel Gabriel taught the Sonship of God.

THEIR TEACHINGS ABOUT THE HOLY SPIRIT

Luke 1:34-35 (The angel Gabriel said to Mary)

34. "How will this be," Mary asked the angel, "since I am a virgin?"

35. "The angel answered, 'The Holy Spirit will come on you, and the power of the Most High will overshadow you. So the holy one to be born will be called the Son of God.'"

The Holy Spirit is God (Acts 5:3-4), not an angel. Hence, the angel said, "The Holy Spirit will come on you."

Quran 16:102 (Surat An-Nahl)

"Say, 'The Holy Spirit [Jibril] has brought it down from your Lord in truth to make firm those who believe and as guidance and good tidings to Muslims.'"

Quran 2:87 (Surat Al-Baqarah)

"And We did certainly give Moses the Scripture and followed up after him with messengers. And We gave Jesus, the son of Mary, clear proofs, and We supported him with the Pure Spirit [Jibril]."

EXPLANATION OF QURAN 2:87

For Muslims, the Holy Spirit is "the angel Jibril," not the one Christians claim to be part of the Trinity. Here, we see the angel Gabriel does not claim to be the Holy Spirit anywhere, but Jibril claims to be the Holy Spirit. Thus, Gabriel is not Jibril.

DID THE ANGEL JIBRIL BRING APOSTLESHIP TO THE JEWS?

Quran 2:97 (Surat Al-Baqarah)

"Say, 'Whoever is an enemy to Jibril—it is [none but] he who has brought the Qur'an down upon your heart, [O Muhammad], by permission of Allah, confirming that which was before it and as guidance and good tidings for the believers.'"

EXPLANATION OF QURAN 2:97

The Jews, in their plots to reject the Prophet Muhammad, asked him, "Which angel brings you revelation?" The Prophet said, "Jibril." They said, "Oh! He is our enemy, we do not want him. If another angel brought you revelation, we would follow you." Jibril did not bring apostleship to the Jews; moreover, this angel Jibril teaches this about the Jews...

Quran 5:82 (Surat Al-Ma'idah)

"You will surely find the most intense of the people in animosity toward the believers [to be] the Jews and those who associate others with Allah..."

Here, we see Jibril teaching Muslims that their greatest enemies are the Jews. To be an enemy of the Jews is to be an enemy of salvation because the Lord Jesus teaches us this...

John 4:19-22 (quoting verse 22 only)

"You worship what you do not know; we worship what we know, for salvation is from the Jews."

Moreover, all the prophets are Jews, from Moses, David, Isaiah, Ezekiel, Daniel, Hosea, Micah, Malachi, John the Baptist, and even Jesus.

DOES THE WAY THE ANGEL GABRIEL APPEARS TO PEOPLE MATCH JIBRIL?

(A) JIBRIL

Quran 19:16-26

16. And mention, [O Muhammad], in the Book [the story of] Mary, when she withdrew from her family to a place toward the east.

17. And she took, in seclusion from them, a screen. Then We sent to her Our Angel, and he represented himself to her as a well-proportioned man.

18. She said, "Indeed, I seek refuge in the Most Merciful from you, [so leave me], if you should be fearing of Allah."

19. He said, "I am only the messenger of your Lord to give you [news of] a pure boy."

20. She said, "How can I have a boy while no man has touched me and I have not been unchaste?"

21. He said, "Thus [it will be]; your Lord says, 'It is easy for Me, and We will make him a sign to the people and a mercy from Us. And it is a matter [already] decreed.'"

22. So she conceived him, and she withdrew with him to a remote place.

23. And the pains of childbirth drove her to the trunk of a palm tree. She said, "Oh, I wish I had died before this and was in oblivion, forgotten."

24. But he called her from below her, "Do not grieve; your Lord has provided beneath you a stream."

25. And shake toward you the trunk of the palm tree; it will drop upon you ripe, fresh dates.

26. So eat and drink and be contented.

HOW JIBRIL APPEARED TO MUHAMMAD:

One day in the month of Ramadan, on the 17th, Monday, in the 40th year of his life, the Prophet saw a man standing before him without seeing where he came from. He said to him, "Read." The Prophet replied, "I do not know how to read; I have not learned." The man grabbed him and squeezed him, then said again, "Read." The Prophet gave the same answer. The third time, the man said, "Read in the name of your Lord who created." He recited that sura to him, and the Prophet recited it back as it was recited to him. This is the first sura revealed in the Quran, although it is not placed at the beginning. The man (angel) then disappeared from his sight, and the Prophet returned home in fear. When he arrived home, his wife Khadija thought he had a fever, so she covered him with blankets. After the fever subsided, he told Khadija everything that had happened, and she comforted him, assuring him that nothing bad would happen to him. Khadija then went to her cousin, Waraka bin Naufal, and told him what had happened to her husband. Waraka said, "That is Jibril who used to come to Prophet Moses and Prophet Jesus. Rejoice, for you are the Prophet of this nation. I wish I were alive to see you lead your people." They returned home, and his fear left him.

This story is found in the book on the life of Prophet Muhammad (S.A.W) written by Sheikh Abdulla Saleh Farsy, the former Chief Kadhi of Zanzibar and later the Chief Kadhi of Kenya, on pages 16-17.

(B) THE ANGEL GABRIEL APPEARING TO PEOPLE DID THIS:

Luke 1:19

He introduced himself by saying, "I am Gabriel."

Daniel 8:15-16

Or the person he appeared to was first informed.

Daniel 8:17-21

Luke 1:13, 30

Gabriel helps the person when they are frightened and says, "Do not be afraid." The characteristics of the angel Gabriel are compassion and gently informing the person, but the angel Jibril of Allah grabs and squeezes the person, which caused Muhammad to have a fever. The question is, who is this Jibril?

WHAT KIND OF BEINGS DOES ALLAH SEND?

Quran 19:83 (Surat Maryam)

"Do you not see that We have sent the devils upon the disbelievers, inciting them to [evil] with [constant] incitement?"

Quran 6:112 (Surat Al-An'am)

"And thus We have made for every prophet an enemy—devils from mankind and jinn, inspiring to one another decorative speech in delusion."

SHETAN (SATAN) CAN TRANSFORM INTO THIS FORM...

2 Corinthians 11:10-15 (quoting verse 14 only)

"And no wonder, for Satan himself masquerades as an angel of light."

"Everyone who acknowledges that Jesus is the Son of God, God lives in them, and the spirit that confesses this is from God (1 John 4:1-3, 15). The angel Gabriel confessed that Jesus is the Son of God, but Jibril did not (Luke 1:35; Quran 9:30). Who is Jibril then?"

WHAT IS THE END FOR THE BEINGS SENT BY ALLAH?

Allah sends devils, and the Holy Scriptures of the Bible teach us the end of these beings like this:

Matthew 25:41

"Then he will say to those on his left

, 'Depart from me, you who are cursed, into the eternal fire prepared for the devil and his angels.'"

Dear beloved, I hope in our Lord Jesus Christ that you have clearly understood that the angel Gabriel of our God Jehovah is not the angel Jibril of Allah, whom Muslims worship.

May the Lord bless you greatly. Spread this message to the nations so they may turn to the Lord Jesus and be saved. Amen!

Today we have learned that Jibril of the Quran is not Gabriel of the Bible.

CHAPTER 04

IS ISA BIN MARYAM AND JESUS CHRIST THE SAME PERSON?

Once again, we thank Jehovah God for granting us this grace to deliver this message of the Bible and its truths to you.

For many years around the world, it has been common to hear Muslims teaching their followers and deceiving them, either unknowingly or knowingly, that Isa bin Maryam, as taught in the Quran, is Jesus Christ.

These teachings are currently being conducted by comparing verses from the Bible and the Quran. Sheikhs, Imams, and many Islamic preachers conduct numerous seminars worldwide. They also use various methods such as pamphlets and recording audio and video tapes, which have caused some half-informed or ignorant Christians to believe that Isa Bin Maryam is Jesus Christ. The fundamental question for all Christians is: Is Isa bin Maryam truly Jesus Christ?

I urge you, in the name of our Lord Jesus Christ, to follow this lesson carefully as we promised in the previous lesson that was given last week.

MAIN SECTIONS OF THIS LESSON

1. Claims used by Muslims to say Isa is Jesus.

2. Is Isa's mother the same as Jesus' mother?

3. The meaning of the name Isa.

4. The meaning of the name Jesus.

5. Is the birth of Jesus the same as Isa's?

6. Is Isa bin Maryam the Son of God?

7. Are the authorities of Isa and Jesus the same?

8. If Jesus is Isa, then Isa…

9. Understand the importance of believing in the Lord Jesus.

Claim No. 1

Muslims say Isa is Jesus.

Quran 3 (Surat Al-Imran) 45:

(Remember) when the angels said, "O Mary, indeed Allah gives you good tidings of a word from Him, whose name will be the Messiah, Jesus, the son of Mary -

distinguished in this world and the Hereafter and among those brought near [to Allah].

Mark 6:3-4:

Is not this the carpenter, the son of Mary and brother of James and Joses and Judas and Simon? And are not his sisters here with us? And they took offense at him. And Jesus said to them, "A prophet is not without honor except in his hometown and among his relatives and in his own household."

Here, Muslims say that just as the Quran teaches the name of Isa's mother is Maryam, similarly, the Bible teaches the name of Jesus' mother is Mary. Therefore, they say that Jesus is Isa.

Also read Matthew 1:18-21 and John 2:1.

Claim No. 2

Isa is a messenger of Allah to the Israelites.

Quran 4 (Surat An-Nisa) 171:

O People of the Scripture, do not commit excess in your religion or say about Allah except the truth. The Messiah, Jesus, the son of Mary, was but a messenger of Allah…

Here we see that the Quran mentions Isa as a messenger. To whom was he sent? Continue reading these verses in the Quran:

Quran 61 (Surat As-Saff) 6:

And [mention] when Jesus, the son of Mary, said, "O children of Israel, indeed I am the messenger of Allah to you confirming what came before me of the Torah and bringing good tidings of a messenger to come after me, whose name is Ahmad."

Also read Quran 3 (Surat Al-Imran) 49:

This verse confirms that Isa is a messenger to the Israelites. To whom was Jesus a messenger? Muslims conducting seminars also read these Bible verses.

Hebrews 3:1:

Therefore, holy brothers, you who share in a heavenly calling, consider Jesus, the apostle and high priest of our confession,

Matthew 15:24:

He answered, "I was sent only to the lost sheep of the house of Israel."

Therefore, just as the Quran teaches that Isa, the son of Mary, is a messenger to the Israelites, so the Bible teaches that Jesus is a messenger to the Israelites. Thus, Isa is Jesus. This is how Islamic preachers teach and hold captive some half-informed Christians. Are these claims true? The Bible will help us answer this later.

Claim No. 3

Isa bin Maryam performed miracles.

Quran 5 (Surat Al-Maidah) 110:

[The Day] when Allah will say, "O Jesus, son of Mary, remember My favor upon you and upon your mother when I supported you with the Pure Spirit and you spoke to the people in the cradle and in maturity; and when I taught you writing and wisdom and the Torah and the Gospel; and when you designed from clay [what was] like the form of a bird with My permission, then you breathed into it, and it became a bird with My permission; and you healed the blind and the leper with My permission; and when you brought forth the dead with My permission; and when I restrained the Children of Israel from [killing] you when you came to them with clear proofs and those who disbelieved among them said, "This is not but obvious magic."

Muslims say this is sufficient evidence as Allah says Isa performed many miracles. Isa healed the blind, just as Jesus healed the blind in Mark 10:46-52. He raised the dead, just as Jesus raised the dead in Mark 5:21-43, and healed the lepers, just as Jesus healed the lepers in Luke 17:1.

Islamic teachers say that just as the Quran narrates that Isa performed many miracles, so does the Bible teach the same. Therefore, Jesus is Isa. Moreover, they say:

Isa bin Maryam is a prophet, Quran 4:171, and similarly, the Bible teaches that Jesus is a prophet, John 6:14, John 7:40, Luke 13:33; 24:19, Mark 6:4, and Matthew 13:57.

According to Bible scholars, it is recorded that Jesus is called a prophet twelve times. Islamic preachers also teach that Isa is an Arabic name, in English Jesus, and in Swahili, Yesu. Through this frequent persuasion, some Christians have been convinced to believe that Isa is Jesus. But, we must scrutinize these claims thoroughly to know the truth.

Let's Investigate Together

1. Is Isa's mother the same as Jesus' mother?

Earlier, we saw that Isa's mother is named Maryam, Quran 3:45, and Jesus' mother is named Mary Matthew 1:18-21, Mark 6:3-4. But the similarity in names cannot necessarily mean they are the same person, as many people share the same name.

The Bible teaches us this:

John 19:25:

But standing by the cross of Jesus were his mother and his mother's sister, Mary the wife of Clopas, and Mary Magdalene.

Here we see three Marys. To identify the difference between Mary, Isa's mother, and Mary, Jesus' mother, we must compare the message of the Quran and the Bible. The Quran narrates about the father and brother of Maryam, Isa's mother, as follows:

Quran 66:12:

And Maryam, the daughter of Imran, who guarded her chastity, so We blew into [her garment] through Our angel, and she believed in the words of her Lord and His scriptures and was of the devoutly obedient.

Quran 19:28:

O sister of Aaron, your father was not a man of evil, nor was your mother unchaste.

Here we see that Maryam, Isa's mother, had a father named Imran and a brother named Aaron.

Reading the Bible, it tells us that Amram fathered:

Numbers 26:59:

And the name of Amram's wife was Jochebed, the daughter of Levi, who was born to Levi in Egypt. And she bore to Amram: Aaron and Moses and Miriam their sister.

Also see 1 Chronicles 6:1-3 and Exodus 6:20.

This Amram lived many years before Jesus, and he was from the lineage of Levi, a descendant of Jacob's son.

Genesis 29:34; Exodus 2:1-10

This is the truth:

If Maryam of the Quran, and Muslims say her father is Imran, then she would have lived 1500 years before Jesus' mother was born!

What lineage does Mary, Jesus' mother, come from?

When we read the Bible, we see that Jesus is called the son of David Matthew 1:1; Mark 10:47 and Luke 1:27,32, which is why Jesus is also called the Lion of Judah Revelation 5:5. Thus, the lineage from which Joseph and Mary, Jesus' mother, came is one.

2. What is the meaning of the name Isa?

It is very common for names to have meanings. For example, these Arabic names mean: Muhammad means "praised one," Abdullah means "servant of Allah," Abu-Bakr means "father of the virgin," Abu Huraira means "father of kittens." Hebrew names also have meanings. Malachi means "my messenger," Isaiah means "salvation of Jehovah," Ezekiel means "God strengthens," Daniel means "God is my judge."

The name Isa means:

In the Quran, which has 30 parts; 114 surahs; 6236 verses; 76,440 words; 322,373 letters; the name Isa is pronounced Isa or Aysi and is mentioned 25 times. Isa is also called the Messiah 93 times. But when we read the Quran translated by Imam Baidawi vol.

1 page 160, it is explained that Isa, an Arabic name, means "reddish with white."

3. What is the meaning of the name Jesus?

The name Jesus is derived from the Hebrew name "Yehoshua," which in Greek is "Iēsous," pronounced "Yesous," meaning Jesus In Arabic, it is "Yasu," in English, "Jesus," meaning "The Lord saves" or "The Lord is salvation"

Isaiah 43:6, 10-11. The Bible, which has a total of 1189 chapters; 31,102 verses; 66 books - 39 in the Old Testament and 27 in the New Testament; the word Savior in English is "Savior" and is mentioned 55 times. Note that in the New Testament, the name Jesus or Yehoshua (in Hebrew) is mentioned 1275 times in about 1226 verses. Also, the New Testament has a total of 7930 verses and 260 chapters. Here we see the name Jesus means Savior and the name Isa means reddish with white. Since the meanings of these names are different, Isa is not the Lord Jesus.

However, Muslims claim he is just an ordinary man and a prophet of Allah as per the Quran,

Surat Al-Maidah 5:75: "The Messiah, son of Mary, was not but a messenger;..."

4. Is the birth of the Lord Jesus the same as Isa?

a) Angel's announcement before their birth, according to the Quran and the Bible:

Jibril appeared to Isa's mother, and Gabriel appeared to Jesus' mother.

Quran says:

He went to Maryam who was in the mosque, Quran 19 (Surat Maryam) 16-17

Isa's pregnancy was only for one day.

Quran 19 (Surat Maryam) 21-22:

(The angel) said: "So it will be; your Lord says, 'It is easy for Me, and We will make him a sign to the people and a mercy from Us. And it is a matter [already] decreed.' So she conceived him, and she withdrew with him to a remote place."

The Bible says:

He went to Mary who was at home, Luke 1:26-28

Quran says:

Maryam, Isa's mother, lived in an unknown village, city, or country. Moreover, the Quran says that Jibril brought the message to the Prophet Muhammad, not to deliver it to the Jews (it was not Jibril's fault) Quran 2 (Surat Al-Baqarah) 97

The Bible says:

Mary, Jesus' mother, was visited by the angel Gabriel in the village of Nazareth in the city of Galilee in the country of Israel Luke 1:26. Mary, Jesus' mother, was a Jew.

Quran says:

Jibril did not greet Mary, Isa's mother, but appeared to her as a perfect human being Quran 19 (Surat Maryam) 17

The Bible says:

The angel Gabriel greeted Mary, Jesus' mother Luke 1:28

Quran says:

Jibril said to Mary, "I am only the messenger of your Lord to give you [news of] a pure boy," Quran 19:19

The Bible says:

The angel Gabriel told Mary, Jesus' mother, that she would conceive a child Luke 1:31

Quran says:

Jibril said to Mary that "We will make him a sign to the people," Quran 19:21. Moreover, Jibril did not mention the child's name to Mary but said, "to give you [news of] a pure boy."

The Bible says:

The angel Gabriel told Mary, Jesus' mother, that the child's name would be Jesus Luke 1:31; 2:21. Gabriel did not say he would give Mary a son but said, "The Holy Spirit will come upon you," meaning the child would be born by the power of God.

b) The difference in the birth of Isa and Jesus is this:

b) Differences in the Birth of Isa and Jesus

- Isa was born under a palm tree (Quran 19:23).

- Jesus was born in a manger (Luke 2:7).

- The duration of Isa's mother's pregnancy is unknown. The angel Jibril said, "I will give you a pure boy," and immediately she conceived and gave birth (Quran 19:22-23).

- When Isa was born, a comforting voice came from beneath the ground (Quran 19:23-24):

"And the pains of childbirth drove her to the trunk of a palm tree. She said, 'Oh, I wish I had died before this and was in oblivion, forgotten.' But he called her from below her, 'Do not grieve; your Lord has provided beneath you a stream.'"

Islamic teachings explain that there is a creature underground that knows the verses of the Quran.

- When Jesus Christ was born, the voices of angels came from above (Luke 2:13-16):

"And suddenly there was with the angel a multitude of the heavenly host praising God and saying, 'Glory to God in the highest, and on earth peace among those with whom he is pleased!' When the angels went away from them into heaven, the shepherds said to one another, 'Let us go over to Bethlehem and see this thing that has happened, which the Lord has made known to us.' And they went with haste and found Mary and Joseph, and the baby lying in a manger."

- But the days for Mary, Jesus' mother, to give birth were fulfilled (Luke 2:6-7).

- The Quran does not show that Isa was foretold by prophets to be born.

- The Bible confirms that prophets foretold the birth of Jesus (Isaiah 7:14; 9:6). This prophecy was given by Prophet Isaiah 750 years before Jesus was born and was fulfilled in Matthew 1:18-2.

- Isa's birthplace is unknown; neither the village, city, nor country is mentioned in the Quran. The Bible informs us that Jesus was born in Bethlehem of Judea in the city of David, five miles south of Jerusalem in Israel (Luke 2:8-16). His birth there also fulfilled the prophecy given by Prophet Micah 750-686 years before Christ, during the reign of these kings, Jotham, Ahaz, and Hezekiah, kings of Judah. Jesus was born around 4 BC during King Herod's reign.

- Isa spoke to people while still an infant, declaring that he was a servant of God, given a book, and made a prophet (Quran 19:30-33).

- Jesus did not speak to anyone as an infant. He began asking questions and giving answers to the elders in the temple at the age of 12 (Luke 2:42-49).

Thus, we see many differences between the Lord Jesus and Isa. Question for you, the follower: Considering the differences in the scriptures of these two books, is Isa bin Maryam the Lord Jesus, the Savior? Reflect on this.

c) Is Isa bin Maryam the Son of God?

If there is one thing that Allah, the God worshipped by Muslims, rejects through the Quran, it is the sonship of God. Allah says this:

Quran 6:101:

He is the Originator of the heavens and the earth. How could He have a son when He does not have a companion? He created all things and has knowledge of all things.

Quran 9:30:

The Jews say, "Uzair is the son of Allah," and the Christians say, "The Messiah is the son of Allah." That is their statement from their mouths; they imitate the saying of those who disbelieved before. May Allah destroy them; how are they deluded?

This is a terrifying directive that Christians and Jews should be destroyed for believing that God has a Son. But Christians believe this because our God:

- Jehovah taught about the Lord Jesus:

Exodus 4:22: "Israel is my firstborn son."

Matthew 17:5: "This is my beloved Son, with whom I am well pleased; listen to him."

- God's angel said this:

Luke 1:30-31, 35:

"And the angel said to her, 'Do not be afraid, Mary, for you have found favor with God. And behold, you will conceive in your womb and bear a son, and you shall call his name Jesus.' The angel answered her, 'The Holy Spirit will come upon you, and the power of the Most High will overshadow you; therefore the child to be born will be called holy—the Son of God.'"

TRUE CHRISTIANS, OUR JESUS CHRIST IS NOT THE ISA OF ISLAM

1. This prophecy is fulfilled in Jesus Christ. We read in Hebrews 7:14:

"For it is evident that our Lord was descended from Judah, and in connection with that tribe Moses said nothing about priests."

But when we read about Isa, his mother comes from the lineage of Imran, who is the father of Aaron, Miriam, and Moses. We read this in Surat Maryam 19:28: "O sister of Aaron, your father was not a man of evil, nor was your mother unchaste."

This explanation, explaining Surat Maryam 19:28, found in the King Fahd Quran translation page 405, reads in English:

"This Harun (Aaron) is not the brother of Musa (Moses), but he was another pious man at the time of Maryam (Mary)."

I, MWAMBA, believe that translating this into Swahili would stand as follows:

"This Harun is not the brother of Moses but another pious man who lived during the period of Maryam."

According to the Bible, Aaron is the child of Amran, and their mother is named Jochebed, they had three children, Aaron, Miriam, and their younger brother Moses. We read this in Numbers 26:59.

2. Another difference is in their creation:

ISA BIN MARYAM WAS CREATED:

Quran 3 (Surat Imran) 59: "Indeed, the example of Jesus to Allah is like that of Adam. He created him from dust; then He said to him, 'Be,' and he was."

JESUS, WAS NOT CREATED BUT IS THE WORD OF GOD:

John 1:1,14:

"In the beginning was the Word, and the Word was with God, and the Word was God... And the Word became flesh and dwelt among us..."

Micah 5:2:

"But you, O Bethlehem Ephrathah, who are too little to be among the clans of Judah, from you shall come forth for me one who is to be ruler in Israel, whose coming forth is from of old, from ancient days."

John 8:58: "Jesus said to them, 'Truly, truly, I say to you, before Abraham was, I am.'"

Furthermore, the Bible tells us that He is the Creator Himself:

John 1:3: "All things were made through him, and without him was not anything made that was made."

Colossians 1:16-17:

"For by him all things were created, in heaven and on earth, visible and invisible, whether thrones or dominions or rulers or authorities—all things were created through him and for him. And he is before all things, and in him all things hold together."

After Living and Dying, Isa bin Maryam of the Muslims Is Claimed to Have Never Appeared to Anyone in Visions!

1. After ascending to heaven, Jesus Christ appeared to many, especially Saul before he became Paul.

Acts 9:4:

"And falling to the ground, he heard a voice saying to him, 'Saul, Saul, why are you persecuting me?' And he said, 'Who are you, Lord?' And he said, 'I am Jesus, whom you are persecuting.'"

Isa bin Maryam Predicted That a Prophet Muhammad Would Come After Him

Quran 61 (Surat As-Saff) 6:

"And [mention] when Jesus, the son of Mary, said, 'O children of Israel, indeed I am the messenger of Allah to you confirming what came before me of the Torah and bringing good tidings of a messenger to come after me, whose name is Ahmad.' But when he came to them with clear evidence, they said, 'This is obvious magic.'"

Jesus Christ Promised a Helper and Sent the Holy Spirit on the Day of Pentecost

John 14:26:

"But the Helper, the Holy Spirit, whom the Father will send in my name, he will teach you all things and bring to your remembrance all that I have said to you."

In Greek, he is called "Paracletos," meaning helper or comforter.

John 15:26:

"But when the Helper comes, whom I will send to you from the Father, the Spirit of truth, who proceeds from the Father, he will bear witness about me."

John 16:7:

"Nevertheless, I tell you the truth: it is to your advantage that I go away, for if I do not go away, the Helper will not come to you. But if I go, I will send him to you."

2. The Name Isa Has No Power
or Ability to Save but Is Associated with Two Colors

In the Hadith Al-Lu'lu'war-Marjan, Volume 1, Hadith number 104, page 64, "Hadith of Ibn Abbas from the Prophet (s.a.w) said:

"I saw Moses on the night of Al-Isra, and he was a tall man with curly hair, resembling the men of Shanu'a. And I saw Jesus, and he was a man of medium build, inclined to redness and whiteness, and his hair was straight…"

But JESUS CHRIST: HIS NAME IS SALVATION: Acts 4:9-10, 12:

"If we are being examined today concerning a good deed done to a crippled man, by what means this man has been healed, let it be known to all of you and to all the people of Israel that by the name of Jesus Christ of Nazareth, whom you crucified, whom God raised from the dead, by him this man is standing before you well… And there is salvation in no one else, for there is no other name under heaven given among men by which we must be saved."

Some verses in the Quran explain that Isa healed the blind. Who are these blind people? Jesus healed the blind, and one of them was Bartimaeus.

Other verses say Isa raised the dead. Who are these? Jesus Christ raised Lazarus.

The name we have been given, which is the only name with salvation, is Jesus Christ. How has the name Isa bin

Maryam, which does not have even a single seed of salvation, been associated with the name of our Jesus Christ?

Acts 16:31: "And they said, 'Believe in the Lord Jesus, and you will be saved, you and your household.'"

I believe that many of you, whether Muslims or not, have already agreed with the scriptures from both sides that Isa bin Maryam is not the Son of God, as we have received evidence in Surat Al-An'am 6:101: "He is the Originator of the heavens and the earth. How could He have a son when He does not have a companion? He created all things and has knowledge of all things."

Quran 9:30 (Surat At-Tawba): "The Jews say, 'Uzair is the son of Allah,' and the Christians say, 'The Messiah is the son of Allah.' That is their statement from their mouths; they imitate the saying of those who disbelieved before. May Allah destroy them; how are they deluded?"

The Teaching of God's Sonship as the Bible Teaches is Not in the Doctrines and Beliefs of the Islamic Religion, Therefore Their Isa is Not the Son of God.

JESUS CHRIST: HE IS THE SON OF GOD

Luke 1:30-31,35:

"And the angel said to her, 'Do not be afraid, Mary, for you have found favor with God. And behold, you will conceive in your womb and bear a son, and you shall call his name Jesus.' The angel answered her, 'The Holy Spirit will come upon you, and the power of the Most High will overshadow you; therefore the child to be born will be called holy—the Son of God.'"

Therefore Isa is Not the Son of God, But Jesus is the Son of God. Hence, Jesus is Not Isa.

3. ISA A.S.: HE IS NOT GOD MADE FLESH

Quran 5:72-73 (Surat Al-Maidah):

Without a doubt, they have disbelieved those who say, "Allah is the Messiah, the son of Mary," while the Messiah has said, "O Children of Israel, worship Allah, my Lord, and your Lord." Indeed, he who associates others with Allah— Allah has forbidden him Paradise, and his refuge is the Fire. And there are not for the wrongdoers any helpers. They have certainly disbelieved those who say, "Allah is the third of three." And there is no god except one God. And if they do not desist from what they are saying, there will surely afflict the disbelievers among them a painful punishment.

JESUS IS THE WORD OF GOD MADE FLESH

John 1:1, 14:

"In the beginning was the Word, and the Word was with God, and the Word was God… And the Word became flesh and dwelt among us…"

4. ISA BIN MARYAM WAS NEITHER CRUCIFIED NOR KILLED

Quran 4:157-158 (Surat An-Nisaa):

"And [for] their saying, 'Indeed, we have killed the Messiah, Jesus, the son of Mary, the messenger of Allah.' And they did not kill him, nor did they crucify him, but [another] was made to resemble him to them. And indeed, those who differ over it are in doubt about it. They have no knowledge of it except the following of assumptions. And they did not kill him, for certain. Rather, Allah raised him to Himself. And ever is Allah Exalted in Might and Wise."

JESUS CHRIST WAS CRUCIFIED ON THE TREE

John 19:18, 31, 33:

"There they crucified him, and with him two others, one on either side and Jesus between them… Since it was the day of Preparation, and so that the bodies would not remain on the cross on the Sabbath (for that Sabbath was a high day), the Jews asked Pilate that their legs might be broken and that they might be taken away… But when they came to Jesus and saw that he was already dead, they did not break his legs."

5. ISA BIN MARYAM DOES NOT DESERVE TO BE WORSHIPED BY ANY HUMAN

Quran 5:116 (Surat Al-Maidah):

"And [beware the Day] when Allah will say, 'O Jesus, son of Mary, did you say to the people, "Take me and my mother as deities besides Allah?"' He will say, 'Exalted are You! It was not for me to say that to which I have no right. If I had said it, You would have known it. You know what is within myself, and I do not know what is within Yourself. Indeed, it is You who is Knower of the unseen.'"

BUT JESUS CHRIST DESERVES TO BE WORSHIPED BY HUMANS AND ANGELS

Matthew 2:2:

"Where is he who has been born king of the Jews? For we saw his star when it rose and have come to worship him."

John 9:35:

"Jesus heard that they had cast him out, and having found him he said, 'Do you believe in the Son of Man?' He answered, 'And who is he, sir, that I may believe in him?' Jesus said to him, 'You have seen him, and it is he who is speaking to you.' He said, 'Lord, I believe,' and he worshiped him."

Philippians 2:10-11:

"So that at the name of Jesus every knee should bow, in heaven and on earth and under the earth, and every tongue confess that Jesus Christ is Lord, to the glory of God the Father."

Hebrews 1:6:

"And again, when he brings the firstborn into the world, he says, 'Let all God's angels worship him.'"

6. ISA BIN MARYAM DOES NOT DESERVE TO BE AN INTERCESSOR FOR PEOPLE TO GOD

Sahih Al-Bukhari, vol.6, Hadith no. 3, The Noble Qur'an, English Translation page 8:

"Go to Moses, the servant of Allah who spoke to Allah directly and was given the Torah. Thus, they will go to him, and he will say, 'I am not fit for the responsibility of intercession,' and he will mention the killing he committed of a person who was not a murderer, and so he will feel ashamed before his Lord, and he will say, 'Go to Jesus, the servant of Allah, His Messenger, His Word, and a spirit from Him.' Isa will say, 'I am not fit for the responsibility of intercession.'"

JESUS CHRIST IS THE INTERCESSOR FOR MANKIND TO GOD

1 Timothy 2:5:

"For there is one God, and there is one mediator between God and men, the man Christ Jesus,"

Hebrews 7:24-25:

"But he holds his priesthood permanently because he continues forever. Consequently, he can save to the uttermost those who draw near to God through him, since he always lives to make intercession for them."

7. ISA BIN MARYAM IS JUST ANOTHER PROPHET, NO DIFFERENT FROM OTHERS

Quran 2:136 (Surat Al-Baqarah):

"Say, 'We have believed in Allah and what has been revealed to us and what has been revealed to Abraham and Ishmael and Isaac and Jacob and the Descendants, and what was given to Moses and Jesus and what was given to the prophets from their Lord. We make no distinction between any of them, and we are Muslims [in submission] to Him.'"

JESUS IS ABOVE ALL THINGS

Ephesians 1:20-23:

"That he worked in Christ when he raised him from the dead and seated him at

his right hand in the heavenly places, far above all rule and authority and power and dominion, and above every name that is named, not only in this age but also in the one to come. And he put all things under his feet and gave him as head over all things to the church, which is his body, the fullness of him who fills all in all."

8. WHEN ISA BIN MARYAM RETURNS, HE WILL MARRY AND HAVE CHILDREN

Mishkat Al-Masabih, vol. 2, page 1159, and Sahih Muslim, vol. 1, page 92 claim that Isa will live for 40 years when he returns, during which he will marry and have children, and he will perform the Hajj.

BUT WHEN JESUS CHRIST RETURNS, HE WILL COME TO TAKE THE CHURCH, HIS BRIDE

Ephesians 5:25-26, 32-33:

"Husbands, love your wives, as Christ loved the church... Therefore a man shall leave his father and mother and hold fast to his wife, and the two shall become one flesh. This mystery is profound, and I am saying that it refers to Christ and the church. However, let each one of you love his wife as himself, and let the wife see that she respects her husband."

Revelation 19:7:

"Let us rejoice and exult and give him the glory, for the marriage of the Lamb has come, and his Bride has made herself ready."

9. ISA WILL DIE AFTER LIVING FOR FORTY YEARS

Mishkat Al-Masabih, vol. 2, page 1159, Sunan Abu Dawud, Hadith no. 4310, Sahih Muslim, vol. 1, page 92 claim that "When Isa returns, he will abolish all religions except Islam. He will destroy the Antichrist (Masih ad-Dajjal) and live on earth for forty years before dying. After his death, he will be buried next to Muhammad."

BUT JESUS CHRIST, AFTER RESURRECTION, LIVES FOREVER AND DOES NOT DIE AGAIN

Romans 6:9:

"We know that Christ, being raised from the dead, will never die again; death no longer has dominion over him."

Hebrews 7:24-25: "But he holds his priesthood permanently because he continues forever. Consequently, he is able to save to the uttermost those who draw near to God through him, since he always lives to make intercession for them."

Revelation 1:17-18:

"When I saw him, I fell at his feet as though dead. But he laid his right hand on me, saying, 'Fear not, I am the first and the last, and the living one. I died, and behold I am alive forevermore, and I have the keys of Death and Hades.'"

10. ISA BIN MARYAM LACKS UNDERSTANDING OF VARIOUS MATTERS

In Al-Lu'lu'war-Marjan, Book 3, Hadith no. 1528, page 883, "Hadith of Abu Huraira from the Prophet says: 'Isa bin Maryam saw a man stealing and asked him, 'Have you stolen?' He replied, 'No, by Allah, besides Whom there is no other god.' Isa said, 'I believe in Allah and I fear my eyes.'"

BUT JESUS KNOWS EVERYTHING

John 1:47-48:

"Jesus saw Nathanael coming toward him and said of him, 'Behold, an Israelite indeed, in whom there is no deceit!' Nathanael said to him, 'How do you know me?' Jesus answered him, 'Before Philip called you, when you were under the fig tree, I saw you.'"

John 2:24-25: "But Jesus on his part did not entrust himself to them, because he knew all people and needed no one to bear witness about man, for he himself knew what was in man."

11. WHEN ISA BIN MARYAM RETURNS, HE WILL BREAK THE CROSSES AND KILL PIGS

Mkweli Mwaminifu, Volumes 3-4, page 20, Hadith no. 753:

"The Hour will not be established until the son of Mary (i.e., Jesus) descends amongst you as a just ruler, and he will break the cross and kill the pigs and abolish the Jizya tax. Wealth will be in such abundance that nobody will accept it."

Also read Sahih Bukhari, vol. 3, Hadith no. 425, and Al-Lu'lu'war-Marjan, vol. 1, Hadith no. 95, page 51.

BUT WHEN JESUS CHRIST RETURNS, HE WILL SEND HIS ANGELS TO GATHER THE SAINTS

Matthew 24:30-31:

"Then will appear in heaven the sign of the Son of Man, and then all the tribes of the earth will mourn, and they will see the Son of Man coming on the clouds of heaven with power and great glory. And he will send out his angels with a loud trumpet call, and they will gather his elect from the four winds, from one end of heaven to the other."

WARNING FROM JESUS CHRIST TO YOU.

Matthew 24:24:

"For false Christs and false prophets will arise and perform great signs and wonders, so as to lead astray, if possible, even the elect." (See also Mark 13:22)

John 8:24:

"I told you that you would die in your sins, for unless you believe that I am he you will die in your sins."

I believe, dear Muslim or anyone who is not in that error and deception, that you have benefited, and if I have offended you in any way, I ask for your forgiveness, as it is not me but the scriptures from both sides.

Muslim, after knowing the truth, I urge you, in the love of Christ, to flee to save your soul in Christ.

Thank you for reading these teachings and the cautions of the Holy Scriptures.

CHAPTER 05

IS ISA BIN MARYAM THE CORRECT NAME OF JESUS IN THE BIBLE?

In this lesson, we will learn about the correct name of Jesus/Yeshua and its translation into Arabic. Is Isa the name of Jesus in the Bible?

The correct historical and translation expert's answer will give us the true meaning of Jesus's name and why he was given that name during the "naming ceremony" (Luke 2:21). This is the name he was called by his mother, his stepfather, his siblings, other relatives, neighbors, friends, and disciples during his lifetime on earth. There is no misunderstanding about the fact that the name Yeshua was not Arabic but Hebrew, and Jesus/Yeshua himself lived in Israel and was born into a devout Jewish family.

The name of Jesus is undoubtedly Hebrew (meaning "salvation"). The translation of the Hebrew name Yeshua into English is Jesus. Jesus's name was not randomly chosen by his parents, but he received his name directly from God (Matthew 1:21, Luke 1:31) because of the meaning of his name and who he was, so today we understand the purpose of Jesus's birth and coming to earth (Matthew 1:21).

In Arab culture and tradition, the name of Jesus is Yasu and not Isa as written in the Islamic Quran. Even today, the name Yasu is used by over 99.99% of all Arab Christians. Visit any Arab church, and you will not hear them using the name Isa. Listen to Arab Christian broadcasts on radio and television (in Arabic), and you will not hear a Christian using the name Isa. Instead, they use the name Yasu. All Christian broadcasts in Arabic use the name Yasu. You will never see the name Isa as it appears in the Muslim Quran.

In Arabic tradition and name translation, the correct Hebrew name (Yeshua) is Yasu in Arabic. Every choice of a foreign name's translation into different languages is a human invention.

Linguistically, it is clear how the Hebrew name Yeshua was translated to Yesu in Swahili and Jesus in English:

Yeshua' (Hebrew) -> Ιησους (Greek) -> Yesu (Latin) -> Jesus (English) -> Yesu (Swahili).

The significant transition is from Hebrew to Greek. This step occurred 200 years before Jesus was born. The translators of the Septuagint (LXX), the classical Greek translation of the Hebrew scriptures, rendered the Hebrew name Yeshua as Ιησους in Greek. The Gospels, written in Greek, adopted this long-established translation tradition.

Because Hebrew and Arabic are two Semitic languages with a close relationship, there are specific rules where Hebrew sounds/words/letters correspond to Arabic sounds/words. Specifically, the Hebrew letter Shin frequently corresponds to Sin in Arabic, for example, the Hebrew word for peace, "shalom," corresponds to the Arabic "salam." According to the linguistic rules and relationships between Hebrew and Arabic, Yasu' is correct in Arabic and Yeshua in Hebrew:

Yeshua' = Yod + Shin + Waw + 'Ain

Yasu' = Ya + Sin + Waw + 'Ain

Again, in correct language, the name Yasu in Arabic corresponds to Yeshua in Hebrew. Thus, in Arab culture and tradition, the name Yasu is accurate and linguistically derived. The transition from Yeshua to Yasu follows the common phonetic change rules from Hebrew to Arabic. Yasu is the Arabic name for Jesus. Conversely, Yasu has its origin in Yeshua.

Early Hebrew (long form): Yehoshua' = Yod + He + Shin + Waw + 'Ain

Later Hebrew (short form): Yeshua' = Yod + Shin + Waw + 'Ain

Arabic (Christian): Yasu' = Ya + Sin + Waw + 'Ain

Arabic (Muslim): 'Isa = 'Ain + Ya + Sin + Ya

"Ya" and "Waw" are weak letters in Arabic, indicating that one can revert to other forms as part of declension or inflection. Thus, one can see that the Islamic form 'Isa is essentially an artificial/human-made inversion (with the change from Waw to Ya). For Arab Christians, the name of Jesus is Yasu and not Isa as written in the Islamic Quran.

I hope today you have learned the difference between the name Jesus in Swahili, Yasu in Arabic, and Yeshua in Hebrew.

CHAPTER 06

HAS MUHAMMAD BEEN PROPHESIED IN THE BIBLE?

Muslims hold that Muhammad was prophesied in the Bible. The main scripture used to support this claim is Deuteronomy 18:18, which states:

"I will raise up for them a prophet like you from among their brothers, and I will put my words in his mouth, and he will tell them everything I command him."

These are the words spoken to Moses by Jehovah.

One of the prominent figures who fervently tried to show that this verse refers to Muhammad was the late Islamic activist Ahmed Deedat from South Africa. When reading or listening to the reasons they provide to prove their claims, they can indeed appear quite compelling (to someone who does not understand the Bible); however, they hold no weight when you know what the Bible says in its entirety and what God's purposes and goals are for the entire lineage of Adam.

One day, Ahmed Deedat confronted a pastor with questions about this verse in Deuteronomy 18:18 to the point that, in his words, Deedat claims the pastor was at a loss for words. When Deedat read this verse to him, he asked, "Who does this prophecy refer to?"

"It refers to Jesus," the pastor replied.

"You know," Deedat said, "The key words in this prophecy are 'like you'. Now, in what way is Jesus like Moses?"

"Moses was a Jew, and Jesus was a Jew. Secondly, Moses was a prophet, and Jesus was a prophet," the pastor replied.

Deedat continues to say, "If these are the only two reasons that help us identify the subject of this prophecy, then this prophecy can refer to any of the following who came after Moses: Solomon, Isaiah, Ezekiel, Daniel, Hosea, Joel, Malachi, John the Baptist, etc., because all of these were Jews and prophets. Why then do you say this prophecy refers to Jesus and not to these others?"

Deedat claims the pastor was left speechless. Then Deedat said, "I believe Jesus does not resemble Moses at all."

The following are the reasons Deedat and other Islamic proponents give to support this claim:

1. Jesus is God (according to the Bible), but Moses is not God. Therefore, he does not resemble Moses.

2. Jesus died for the sins of the world (according to the Bible), but Moses did not die for that purpose. Therefore, he does not resemble Moses.

3. Jesus went to hell for three days (according to the Bible), but Moses did not go there. Therefore, he does not resemble Moses.

Deedat then continued to show how Moses resembles Muhammad. Here are his or their Muslim arguments:

1. Moses and Muhammad had both a father and a mother, but Jesus did not have a human father. Therefore, the one who resembles Moses is Muhammad, not Jesus.

2. Moses and Muhammad were born in the usual way, but Jesus was created through a miraculous act.

3. Moses and Muhammad married and had children, but Jesus neither married nor had children during his life.

4. Moses and Muhammad were accepted as prophets by their contemporaries, but Jesus was rejected. Even today, the Jews do not accept him. The Bible itself says: He came to his own, and his own people did not receive him (John 1:11).

5. Moses and Muhammad were both prophets and kings. They were prophets because they received revelation from God and conveyed it to God's creatures. They were kings because they had the authority of life and death over their people. For example, Moses ordered the execution of a man caught gathering sticks on the Sabbath (Numbers 15:32-36). Muhammad also had such authority. Other prophets like Jonah, Daniel, Ezra, etc., had the gift of prophecy but did not have the authority to take a person's life. Jesus also belonged to this second group. Therefore, he does not resemble Moses.

6. Moses and Muhammad brought new laws to their people. But Jesus did not bring new laws. Even he himself admitted that: "Do not think that I have come to abolish the Law or the Prophets; I have not come to abolish them but to fulfill them. For truly, I say to you, until heaven and earth pass away, not an iota, not a dot, will pass from the Law until all is accomplished." (Matthew 5:17-18).

7. Moses and Muhammad died natural deaths, but according to Christianity, Jesus was killed brutally on the cross.

8. Moses and Muhammad died and are buried, but according to Christianity, Jesus is in heaven.

Deedat says, "The pastor had no defense; I told him, 'Here I have proved to you just one thing. But the prophecy says more than that. There is a part that says the prophet will come, 'from among their brothers.'"

So he continued his arguments:

9. Abraham had two sons. Ishmael from Hagar, and Isaac from Sarah. These were brothers. The children of Isaac are Jews, and the children of Ishmael are Arabs. Therefore, the children of Ishmael are the brothers of the children of Isaac. If the prophet was to come from among their brothers, then it was for the Arabs and not for the Jews themselves. Muhammad, who is a descendant of Ishmael, is the prophet among the brothers of the Jews, i.e., the Arabs, mentioned in Deuteronomy 18:18, and not Jesus, who is a Jew. Doesn't the Bible itself say about Ishmael: "They lived from Havilah to Shur, which is opposite Egypt in the direction of Assyria. He settled over against all his kinsmen." (Genesis 25:18)?

10. The prophecy says: "I will put my words in his mouth." This is Muhammad because he was illiterate, that is, he had not studied, but when the angel Gabriel appeared to him in the cave of Hira (or Jabal-un Noor), he told him 'iqra' or 'read' or 'say'. As a result, Muhammad began to say the words that Allah was placing in his mouth for the next 23 years – which have now become the Quran.

11. The prophet Isaiah says: "And the book is given to one who cannot read, saying, 'Read this,' he says, 'I cannot

read.'" (Isaiah 29:12). This passage refers to Muhammad because when he was receiving the message from Allah, he was an uneducated person except for what came from Allah himself.

12. The prophecy continues: "I myself will call to account anyone who does not listen to my words that the prophet speaks in my name." (Deuteronomy 18:19). Deedat says that the Quran in surah Nas, verse 114, begins by saying: "In the name of God, most gracious, most merciful." Also, every chapter following it, that is, 112, 111, 110, etc., begins the same way. Therefore, what Muhammad says, he does in the name of Allah – just as the prophecy of Deut. 18:19 says. "But," Deedat says, "Christians begin with 'In the name of the Father, the Son, and the Holy Spirit.'"

These arguments, when examined, are very strong and, in normal circumstances, have great logic. These are arguments that can entirely pull someone away from eternal life in Christ and plunge them into eternal destruction. And I believe they may have already done so for some people.

I don't know, dear reader, what you would say if you were faced with these arguments. How strong would your faith remain after encountering such heavy arguments?

You can read these arguments in English by clicking HERE.

So, I ask you to follow me in the second part of this article, where I will explain how these arguments have no scriptural truth despite appearing so weighty.

Jesus Christ is the way, the truth, and the life. Jesus Christ is the ark of these times. A flood is coming, where everyone outside the ark will be swept away by eternal fire.

The Apostle Paul says it very well:

"And my speech and my message were not in plausible words of wisdom, but in demonstration of the Spirit and of power, so that your faith might not rest in the wisdom of men but in the power of God. Yet among the mature we do impart wisdom, although it is not a wisdom of this age or of the rulers of this age, who are doomed to pass away. But we impart a secret and hidden wisdom of God, which God decreed before the ages for our glory. None of the rulers of this age understood this, for if they had, they would not have crucified the Lord of glory. But, as it is written, 'What no eye has seen, nor ear heard, nor the heart of man imagined, what God has prepared for those who love him'—these things God has revealed to us through the Spirit. For the Spirit searches everything, even the depths of God. For who knows a person's thoughts except the spirit of that person, which is in him? So also no one comprehends the thoughts of God except the Spirit of God. Now we have received not the spirit of the world, but the Spirit who is from God, that we might understand the things freely given us by God. And we impart this in words not taught by human wisdom but taught by the Spirit, interpreting spiritual truths to those who are spiritual. The natural person does not accept the things of the Spirit of God, for they are folly to him, and he is not able to understand them because they are spiritually discerned. The spiritual person judges all things, but is himself to be judged by no one." (1 Corinthians 2:4-15).

Hold firmly to what you have so that no one may take your crown, for the days we live in are times of great evil.

But We Did Not Receive the Spirit of the World, But the Spirit From God

But we did not receive the spirit of the world, but the Spirit who is from God, so that we may understand what God has freely given us. And this we speak, not in words taught by human wisdom, but in words taught by the Spirit, explaining spiritual realities with Spirit-taught words.

The natural person does not accept the things of the Spirit of God, for they are folly to him, and he is not able to understand them because they are spiritually discerned. But the spiritual person judges all things, yet is himself to be judged by no one. (1 Corinthians 2:12-15).

One major issue I often see in Islam and among Muslims is the focus on physical things. This becomes a significant problem when dealing with spiritual matters.

If you are on a life journey in the physical world and aim to end up in the spiritual world (which is the ultimate destiny for all human beings), then you must seek the meaning of physical matters according to the spiritual realm. If you only look at things from a physical perspective, you suffer a great loss!!

It is crucial to recognize that God does not give us His message to make us rich, famous, and influential here on earth. If these are your main goals in this life, then you are at a greater loss than anyone. These are not the primary concerns. God has placed us on earth for much greater purposes. He focuses on eternal matters, not temporary ones. Therefore, the core of God's true message is the eternal life to come in the spiritual world.

Now, since my dear brothers focus more on worldly, physical matters, it is not surprising to see Ahmed Deedat and his colleagues end up looking at the physical characteristics of Moses and comparing them with the physical characteristics of Muhammad, claiming that this is proof that the Bible verses they quote refer to Muhammad.

It is very sad to see such great effort ultimately leading to destruction. And it is even more tragic because there is a long line of people behind them who believe in Deedat and his peers.

However, I am entirely convinced that their innermost intentions are very good. They are people who have wholeheartedly dedicated themselves to their God and their religion. The only question remains, are they correct?

But whenever you see these brothers striving to justify Islam, even through the Bible, you truly feel sympathy for them. They are genuinely struggling. Psychologically, it shows signs of a person who is constantly being tormented by their conscience over something that their soul does not accept but tries every way to suppress the reality to find some inner peace.

Have you ever seen someone who has gone through a significant loss, for example, losing a close loved one? Because the soul refuses to accept this reality, they start saying many things. For instance, they might say, "It's impossible! Musa, we were just with him yesterday. Musa was such a good person. Why should he die? This isn't right. No, Musa is still here. These are just people's conspiracies!" etc., etc.

This person will struggle while their soul desperately wishes the event hadn't happened but was as they wished. But what is the end result? They will eventually have to accept it.

This is what I interpret for these brothers who are making great efforts to justify their Prophet through the Bible. But it will never be possible! If you reject the truth, any effort to justify falsehood will not produce the fruits you expect; even if your intentions are good. Good intentions do not turn falsehood into truth, not even once!

And it is very surprising that their God told them that the Prophet was mentioned in the Bible, which is not true at all! This alone is enough to make any Muslim who seeks eternal life question twice. The only problem is that they have been taught to fear questioning and scrutinizing things.

The Quran says that Allah will have mercy on various people, including:

"...those that shall follow the Apostle – the Unlettered Prophet – whom they shall find mentioned in the Torah and the Gospel." (Sura 7:157).

In general translation, it says he will also have mercy on those (Christians) who follow the Prophet (Muhammad) who is mentioned in the Torah and the Gospel (the Bible). Yes! That's what it says.

Maybe they will say that this verse has been added by people – which they cannot claim because they are quick to argue that the Bible has been altered and corrupted, but not the Quran.

Because of this verse, Muslims have made great efforts to find where in the Torah and the Gospel Muhammad is mentioned as Allah told them.

Now their efforts and diligence have fallen on several scriptures, including Deuteronomy 18:18 and Isaiah 29:12. Therefore, they have presented many arguments (which, as I said, are purely physical) to try and fulfill their desire to see that what their God told them is indeed found in the Bible. [Muslims, wake up; reflect; question what you believe].

If you haven't read their arguments, please see the first part of this article.

What makes these Muslim arguments lack logic?

Even Swahili speakers say that the secret of the pitcher is known by the cutter. Jehovah, who is the owner of the Bible, we have seen that He says in Corinthians that we speak words taught by the Spirit, explaining spiritual realities with Spirit-taught words.

The one who owns the Word has placed a standard for His Word – that if you want to understand what He means, you must interpret His Word spiritually. It would be strange if you, an outsider, came with your own rules for running someone else's household that the owner did not set.

Then you expect others not to believe the homeowner but to believe you!

This world is passing away. In the coming days, this world along with everything we see in the sky will cease to exist. Instead, there will be a new eternal world.

God, in His dealings with humanity, focuses on eternal matters. These things about food, clothes, wives, husbands, etc., are just things of this world that enable us to live here to reach the ultimate goal – to live ETERNALLY!

All things God speaks of in the Bible are aimed at that future eternal life. This means they focus on the coming spiritual world; not this physical world.

God uses our physical lives to prepare our future spiritual lives. Also, He used the physical lives of the nation and people of Israel to convey the message of spiritual matters. The Bible is a historical book about the nation of Israel. The Bible is a book with a message of current and future spiritual realities presented through the physical lives of the nation of Israel.

Therefore, if you read the Bible and end up seeing only that:

- There was a man called Pharaoh.

- There were people called Israelites. They were slaves in Egypt and later left for Israel.

- The Jews wandered in the desert and some died there.

- Moses had a wife.

- Noah lived and built an ark. Many people died in the flood.

- Jesus took off his shoes whenever he entered the synagogue.

- The Jews circumcised their children.

- The Jews washed their hands before eating.

- The Jews kept beards.

- Moses died like other humans, etc., etc.

If these are the only things you see, you are no different from a primary or secondary school student studying the History of past events. There you have never realized that God is not a history teacher or writer. Teaching History is not something God concerns Himself with, not even a little. Not at all!!

My Muslim brothers, God is engaged in a work that determines LIFE and DEATH for humans. God's message is about where every human being will be ETERNALLY! Is it in heaven forever; or in hell forever?

You must go beyond the physical level of viewing things and enter the spiritual level. Only then will you begin to speak of matters of God who is Spirit; and not flesh and blood like us humans. It is crucial to seek the eternal message within the temporal message.

Let's read again the scripture from the Bible that Muslims use to justify their Prophet:

"I will raise up for them a prophet like you from among their brothers, and I will put my words in his mouth, and he will tell them everything I command him." (Deuteronomy 18:18).

We will examine this verse step by step and how it never refers to Muhammad.

The Words 'from among their brothers'

Jehovah told Moses that He would bring a prophet to Israel from among their brothers.

It is very clear that in this scripture, the God of Israel is referring to a specific prophet, despite the fact that Israel had many prophets. Therefore, for it not to apply to every prophet, this prophet must be different from the others in how he would resemble Moses. Ahmed Deedat and his Muslim colleagues claim that this prophet is Muhammad based on the reasons we saw in the first part of this article.

Let's start by laying the foundation. God set a rule concerning the rulers of Israel. The rule says that:

"When you enter the land the Lord your God is giving you and have taken possession of it and settled in it, and you say, 'Let us set a king over us like all the nations around us,' be sure to appoint over you the king the Lord your God chooses. He must be from among your own brothers. Do not place a foreigner over you, one who is not an Israelite." (Deuteronomy 17:14-15).

Ahmed Deedat claims that the words 'their brothers' in Deuteronomy 18:18 mean the descendants of Ishmael (i.e., Arabs). In the centuries and centuries of Israelite rulers, when has there ever been an Israelite king who was an Ishmaelite (Arab)? The answer is NEVER!

This scripture alone is enough to completely disqualify Muhammad in relation to Deut. 18:18. However, let's continue.

Let's look at the following

 scriptures:

- "But the Benjamites would not listen to their fellow Israelites." (Judges 20:13)

- "Then it shall be, when their fathers or their brothers come to us to complain, that we will say to them, 'Be kind to them for our sakes, because we did not take a wife for any of them in the war; for it is not as though you had given the women to them at this time, making yourselves guilty of your oath.'" (Judges 21:22)

- "Then Abner called to Joab and said, 'Must the sword devour forever? Do you not know that the end will be bitter? How long will you keep from turning from pursuing your brothers?'" (2 Samuel 2:26)

- "Now the men and their wives raised a great outcry against their fellow Jews." (Nehemiah 5:1)

- "But they shall assist their brothers in performing their duties at the tent of meeting, but they themselves shall not do the service. Thus, you shall do to the Levites concerning their duties." (Numbers 8:26).

- "The children you will have after them will be yours; in the territory they inherit, they will be reckoned under the names of their brothers." (Genesis 48:6).

- "But to the half-tribe of Manasseh, Moses had given a heritage in Bashan; but to the other half Joshua gave among their brothers, on this side of Jordan westward." (Joshua 22:7).

These scriptures mention the words 'their brothers.' But all of them refer to Israelites, not Arabs. What I want to show here is that the words 'their brothers' are used many times in the Bible. Although there are a few instances where they refer to the descendants of Ishmael, generally they refer to the Israelites themselves.

And the good thing is that in the same Deuteronomy 18 which Muslims quote, the words are used. God explains about the tribe of Levi being priests. He says: "They shall have no inheritance among their fellow Israelites; the Lord is their inheritance, as he promised them." (Deut. 18:2). Do Ahmed Deedat and his colleagues also want to tell us that they were not to have an inheritance among the Arabs?

In short, the prophet was prophesied to come from one of the tribes of Israel and not from outside. Jesus Christ came from the tribe of Judah.

The Words 'like you'

How is Jesus Christ like Moses? As I said, God conveys a spiritual message, not a physical one, in the Bible. The following are just some comparisons between Moses and Jesus:

- Moses left his wealthy and royal life in Pharaoh's house to live with his poor and enslaved Israeli brothers. It is written:

"By faith Moses, when he had grown up, refused to be known as the son of Pharaoh's daughter. He chose to be mistreated along with the people of God rather than to enjoy the fleeting pleasures of sin. He regarded disgrace for the sake of Christ as of greater value than the treasures of Egypt, because he was looking ahead to his reward." (Hebrews 11:24-26).

Jesus also left his great glory in heaven. It is written:

"In your relationships with one another, have the same mindset as Christ Jesus: Who, being in very nature God, did not consider equality with God something to be used to his own advantage; rather, he made himself nothing by taking the very nature of a servant, being made in human likeness. And being found in appearance as a man, he humbled himself by becoming obedient to death – even death on a cross!" (Philippians 2:5-8).

- Moses was sent by God to deliver Israel from the land of bondage under Pharaoh and their oppressors to take them to the promised land. Jesus was sent by God to deliver humanity from the bondage of the devil (the spiritual Pharaoh) to take them to heaven.

- Moses was a mediator between the children of Israel and God when they sinned. His prayers averted God's plagues. Jesus is the mediator between God and humans. He intercedes for those who believe in Him so that they ultimately do not end up in the fire of hell.

- Moses redeemed the children of Israel from the bondage of Egypt through the sacrifice of blood. The Israelites were instructed to slaughter the Passover lamb and put its blood on the doorposts of their houses. Then the Bible says:

"The blood will be a sign for you on the houses where you are, and when I see the blood, I will pass over you. No destructive plague will touch you when I strike Egypt.

When the Lord goes through the land to strike down the Egyptians, he will see the blood on the top and sides of the doorframe and will pass over that doorway, and he will not permit the destroyer to enter your houses and strike you down." (Exodus 12:13, 23).

Jesus also redeemed all humanity from the bondage of Satan through the sacrifice of blood. The Bible says:

"But when Christ came as high priest of the good things that are now already here, he went through the greater and more perfect tabernacle that is not made with human hands, that is to say, is not a part of this creation. He did not enter by means of the blood of goats and calves; but he entered the Most Holy Place once for all by his own blood, thus obtaining eternal redemption." (Hebrews 9:11-12).

- Moses instructed the Israelites to gather manna that fell in the desert every day to eat and live in the desert. It is written:

"Each morning everyone gathered as much as they needed." (Exodus 16:21).

Since these were signs of things to come, when the Lord of life Himself came, Jesus Christ, He brought the real substance that was awaited. It is written:

"Our ancestors ate the manna in the wilderness; as it is written: 'He gave them bread from heaven to eat.' Jesus said to them, 'Very truly I tell you, it is not Moses who has given you the bread from heaven, but it is my Father who gives you the true bread from heaven. For the bread of God is the bread that comes down from heaven and gives life to the world.'" (John 6:31-33).

- The people were bitten by snakes in the desert. God told Moses to make a bronze snake. He raised it up so that anyone bitten by a snake could look up at the bronze snake and be healed. Those who did so lived. Those who did not died. It is written:

"So Moses made a bronze snake and put it up on a pole. Then when anyone was bitten by a snake and looked at the bronze snake, they lived." (Numbers 21:9).

Jesus did the same thing. The snake represents the devil and all demons. Being bitten by a snake represents having sin. Everyone with sin must look at Jesus with faith, and they will be healed from death – that is, not be thrown into the fire of hell. Those who refuse to look at Jesus choose to die! It is written:

"Just as Moses lifted up the snake in the wilderness, so the Son of Man must be lifted up, that everyone who believes may have eternal life in him." (John 3:14-15).

- Moses was rejected by his own people. They said to him: "Who made you ruler and judge over us? Are you thinking of killing me as you killed the Egyptian?" Then

Moses was afraid and thought, "What I did must have become known." (Exodus 2:14).

Then he left and went to the land of Midian. There he married a wife who was not an Israelite. (See: Ex. 2:16-21). But later he returned to Egypt and led the Israelites out of bondage.

Jesus was also rejected by his own people. It is written: "He came to that which was his own, but his own did not receive him." (John 1:11). It is clear that to this day, the Jews do not recognize Jesus as their Messiah. But like Moses, the Lord Jesus turned from his own people and went to the Gentiles, that is, all the people who are not Jews. There he has been gathering and continues to gather a 'bride' – for the Church of Jesus, in its entirety, is called the bride of the Lord Jesus (See 2 Corinthians 11:2). And it is written again: "I will call them 'my people' who are not my people; and I will call her 'my loved one' who is not my loved one." (Romans 9:25).

But before entering Canaan (the end of the world), the Lord Jesus, like Moses, will return to Israel. It is written: "I do not want you to be ignorant of this mystery, brothers and sisters, so that you may not be conceited: Israel has experienced a hardening in part until the full number of the Gentiles has come in, and in this way all Israel will be saved. As it is written: 'The deliverer will come from Zion; he will turn godlessness away from Jacob.'" (Romans 11:25-26).

- Moses appointed twelve men and sent them to Canaan. It is written: "The plan pleased me well; so I took twelve of your men, one man from each tribe." (Deuteronomy 1:23). The Lord Jesus also appointed twelve apostles and sent them. It is written: "He appointed twelve that they might be with him and that he might send them out to preach." (Mark 3:14).

- Moses appointed seventy people to stand before the Lord. It is written: "The

Lord said to Moses: 'Bring me seventy of Israel's elders who are known to you as leaders and officials among the people. Have them come to the tent of meeting, that they may stand there with you.'" (Numbers 11:16). The Lord Jesus did the same. It is written: "After this the Lord appointed seventy others and sent them two by two ahead of him to every town and place where he was about to go." (Luke 10:1).

- Moses was a priest. It is written: "Moses and Aaron were among his priests, Samuel was among those who called on his name; they called on the Lord and he answered them." (Psalm 99:6). The Lord Jesus is also a priest. It is written about Him: "But because Jesus lives forever, he has a permanent priesthood." (Hebrews 7:24).

- Moses gave his people water in the desert. It is written: "Then Moses raised his arm and struck the rock twice with his staff. Water gushed out, and the community and their livestock drank." (Numbers 20:11). Jesus does the same thing. It is written: "On the last and greatest day of the festival, Jesus stood and said in a loud voice, 'Let anyone who is thirsty come to me and drink.'" (John 7:37).

- Moses bore the sins of his people and was punished for them. It is written: "By the waters of Meribah they angered the Lord, and trouble came to Moses because of them." (Psalm 106:32). Everyone knows that our Lord Jesus also bore the sins of the whole world. He was punished on our behalf. It is written: "But he was pierced for our transgressions, he was crushed for our iniquities; the punishment that brought us peace was on him, and by his wounds we are healed. We all, like sheep, have gone astray, each of us has turned to our own way; and the Lord has laid on him the iniquity of us all." (Isaiah 53:5-6).

We could go on and on, but these few examples are enough to show that indeed Moses was a type of the prophet who was to come. He was a type because he was fulfilling his duty physically, while the awaited One would fulfill it spiritually, which is indeed God's ultimate purpose.

The Words 'I will put my words in his mouth'

The prophet Jeremiah says: "Then the Lord reached out his hand and touched my mouth and said to me, 'I have put my words in your mouth.'" (Jeremiah 1:9). So, if

Deuteronomy 18:18 concerns a prophet in whom God put His words, why should we think it refers to Muhammad, a distant foreigner, and not to Jeremiah who is an Israelite?

What about Isaiah? It is written: "I have put my words in your mouth and covered you with the shadow of my hand—I who set the heavens in place, who laid the foundations of the earth, and who say to Zion, 'You are my people.'" (Isaiah 51:16).

Every true prophet of God spoke the words that God put within them. They were not their own words; nor were they words learned in schools or colleges. They were words spoken by the Spirit of God from within them. In short, these words do not identify Muhammad at all. Why not Jeremiah? Why not Isaiah?

But what does the Lord Jesus say? "For I gave them the words you gave me and they accepted them. They knew with certainty that I came from you, and they believed that you sent me." (John 17:8).

So, just as Deedat challenged the pastor that being Jewish and a prophet could refer to any prophet, not necessarily Jesus, the same principle applies to him. Having words put in one's mouth could refer to any prophet and is not evidence that the one spoken of is Muhammad. And it is unimaginable that God, who spent thousands of years preparing this chosen nation, would end up placing a foreigner over them!!

The Words 'I do not know'

The prophet Isaiah wrote: "Or if you give the scroll to someone who cannot read and say, 'Read this, please,' they will answer, 'I don't know how to read.'" (Isaiah 29:12).

When Muslims saw this verse, they thought they had found proof that Muhammad is mentioned in the Bible because Muhammad was an unlettered person.

If you follow the entire chapter 29 and the context that produced this verse 12, you might end up laughing, although this is not a laughing matter.

What Muslims are doing is a great distortion that destroys millions of God's people eternally in the fire of hell. People are made to believe lies, and they embrace them as if they are the truth.

Overall, if you read chapter 29, it is a chapter that pronounces judgment on Ariel (Jerusalem) because of their rebellion against God's laws and commandments. Let's read the chapter closely:

1. "Woe to you, Ariel, Ariel, the city where David settled! Add year to year and let your cycle of festivals go on.

2. Yet I will besiege Ariel; she will mourn and lament, she will be to me like an altar hearth.

3. I will encamp against you on all sides; I will encircle you with towers and set up my siege works against you.

4. Brought low, you will speak from the ground; your speech will mumble out of the dust. Your voice will come ghostlike from the earth; out of the dust your speech will whisper.

5. But your many enemies will become like fine dust, the ruthless hordes like blown chaff. Suddenly, in an instant,

6. the Lord Almighty will come with thunder and earthquake and great noise, with windstorm and tempest and flames of a devouring fire.

7. Then the hordes of all the nations that fight against Ariel, that attack her and her fortress and besiege her, will be as it is with a dream, with a vision in the night—

8. as when a hungry person dreams of eating, but awakens hungry still; as when a thirsty person dreams of drinking, but awakens faint and thirsty still. So will it be with the hordes of all the nations that fight against Mount Zion.

9. Be stunned and amazed, blind yourselves and be sightless; be drunk, but not from wine, stagger, but not from beer.

10. The Lord has brought over you a deep sleep: He has sealed your eyes (the prophets); he has covered your heads (the seers)."

The words in red ink are the judgments themselves. Besides the judgments above, God also said that because of their rebellion, they would not understand His word. They would not hear or know what God was saying even if they read or heard His word. This includes those expected to understand this word – the prophets and seers – not to mention those without knowledge of God's word, the common people. Therefore, He continues to say:

11. "For you this whole vision is nothing but words sealed in a scroll. And if you give the scroll to someone who can read, and say, 'Read this, please,' they will answer, 'I can't; it is sealed.'

12. Or if you give the scroll to someone who cannot read and say, 'Read this, please,' they will answer, 'I don't know how to read.'"

So, if Muhammad is indeed the one mentioned in Isaiah 29:12, it logically means he is among those who understand nothing because they are under God's judgment; because as we have seen, this chapter is a pronouncement of God's judgment due to rebellion. Not bad though! That is why I said that reading this Muslim argument might make you laugh.

However, since Muhammad is a prophet who understands nothing due to being under God's judgment according to the logic of this verse, it means the message he brought to humanity does not come from the God who created heaven and earth. Yes! Unless, deliberately, you refuse the existing logic. Why then follow such a person?

Dear Muslims, my question here is just one. Anyone who loves the truth will recognize that Deuteronomy 18:18 or Isaiah 29:12 do not refer to Muhammad at all despite the attempts of Islamic scholars to tell you otherwise.

One major problem with any form of knowledge is when you are a person who swallows everything you are told without investigating the truth of the matters. Even what I have told you in this article, it would be better not to just swallow it. Conduct your own investigation into the truth and falsehood of the arguments from both sides. If the scholars are telling the truth, then hold on to it. If this article is telling the truth, then wrestle with your fear and reject the falsehood.

Now, my question is, if Allah indeed said that Muhammad is mentioned in the Torah and the Gospel when it is not true, what does that mean? The work is on you!

Jesus loves you. Come to Jesus while there is still time. There is no salvation outside of Jesus. All your efforts to try to please God without Jesus, I am one hundred percent sure, will fail. And every time you try, you find yourself being consumed by guilt and fear in your heart. You are not ready to confess this openly, but you cannot deceive your heart. Your heart knows very well that you have failed miserably!

And the more you continue to reject Jesus, that failure to live a holy life will be your portion until the end.

Jesus loves you VERY MUCH! He died for you. Come to Jesus now.

CHAPTER 07

IS MUHAMMAD OR GABRIEL THE SPIRIT OF TRUTH/HOLY SPIRIT?

In this Chapter, I will answer all Muslims worldwide using the Holy Bible to show that Muhammad was not the Spirit of Truth as promised by Jesus Christ, who is our Lord and Savior.

Often, Muslims ask, "Who is the Spirit of Truth that Jesus promised in John 16:12-14?" I have been asking Muslims who they think this Spirit of Truth is, and they respond that the Spirit of Truth is the Angel Gabriel.

John 16:13 says: "But when he, the Spirit of truth, comes, he will guide you into all the truth. He will not speak on his own; he will speak only what he hears, and he will tell you what is yet to come."

Moreover, many Muslims claim that Jesus was prophesying about Muhammad, while others say he was prophesying about Gabriel. CONTRARY to this, as evidenced in John 16:13, Jesus was speaking about the Holy Spirit. We know this because Jesus refers to the Spirit who would guide his disciples from that moment on, not hundreds of years later.

If you carefully read the Bible from John 16:5-15, you will immediately realize that all Muslims and their Allah are liars.

There are many ways we can understand if Muslims are right in their interpretation by looking at or reading every time Jesus mentioned the "Spirit" in the Gospel of John and see if he was truly prophesying about Muhammad in any of these verses.

First Evidence:

John 1:32 says: "Then John gave this testimony: 'I saw the Spirit come down from heaven as a dove and remain on him [JESUS].'"

We all know that Muhammad was not holy and did not descend like a bird, and he came 600 years after Christ. Therefore, it is clear that the Holy Spirit is not Muhammad who came 600 years later. John never saw Muhammad.

Second Evidence:

John 1:33 [John the Baptist continues saying]: "And I myself did not know him, but the one who sent me to baptize with water told me, 'The man on whom you see the Spirit come down and remain is the one who will baptize with the Holy Spirit.'"

John makes it clearer that Jesus is the one who will baptize with the Holy Spirit.

In short, Jesus will send the SPIRIT who is God's Power and is God.

Is Muhammad that Spirit? ABSOLUTELY NOT, because Jesus baptized his disciples, and moreover, his followers were baptized with the Holy Spirit on the day of Pentecost. This happened shortly after Jesus ascended to his Father in Heaven, which was 600 years before Muhammad was born. The disciples of Jesus were not baptized through Muhammad, nor do Muslims baptize.

Third Evidence:

John 3:5 says: "Jesus answered, 'Very truly I tell you, no one can enter the kingdom of God unless they are born of water and the Spirit.'"

I am sure no Muslim in the world can say that Muhammad gives birth, because in the above verse, Jesus says one must be born of the Spirit. DID MUHAMMAD GIVE BIRTH/DOES HE GIVE BIRTH?

Fourth Evidence:

John 3:6 says: "Flesh gives birth to flesh, but the Spirit gives birth to spirit."

Here Muhammad is immediately excluded because of these words that Jesus said, because 1 Muhammad was a human being, and even worse, he is now dead. And 2 the Spirit gives birth using the Power of God, which is the Holy Spirit. This spiritual birth began 600 years before Muhammad was born.

Fifth Evidence:

John 3:8 says: "The wind blows wherever it pleases. You hear its sound, but you cannot tell where it comes from or where it is going. So it is with everyone born of the Spirit."

NONE OF US WAS BORN THROUGH MUHAMMAD.

Therefore, Muhammad fails again to be the Spirit of Truth.

Sixth Evidence:

John 3:34 says: "For the one whom God has sent speaks the words of God, for God gives the Spirit without limit."

Was Muhammad unlimited? Here again, Muhammad fails because he was limited in words by his Allah. Muhammad admitted that he did not know what Allah would do to him after death, when people asked him what would happen after death. Muhammad was not "omniscient."

Seventh Evidence:

John 4:24 says: "God is spirit, and his worshipers must worship in the Spirit and in truth."

God is not Muhammad. Thank God, for making it clear that the Holy Spirit is God. Therefore, even Gabriel is not the Holy Spirit.

Eighth Evidence:

John 6:63 says: "The Spirit gives life; the flesh counts for nothing. The words I have spoken to you—they are full of the Spirit and life."

Muhammad cannot give eternal life, which is something only God can give. That is why we know that Jesus is God because Jesus gives eternal life to all who believe in Him.

Ninth Evidence:

John 7:39 says: "By this, he meant the Spirit, whom those who believed in him were later to receive. Up to that time, the Spirit had not been given, since Jesus had not yet been glorified."

Will Muhammad be given to everyone who believes in Jesus? ABSOLUTELY NOT, the Quran says that if you believe in Muhammad/Allah, then you believe in Allah. Therefore, Muhammad cannot be the Spirit of Truth because we who believe in Jesus have been given the Holy Spirit, not Muhammad who is already dead.

Tenth Evidence:

John 14:16-18 says: "16 And I will ask the Father, and he will give you another advocate to help you and be with you forever—17 the Spirit of truth. The world cannot accept him, because it neither sees him nor knows him. But you know him, for he lives with you and will be in you. 18 I will not leave you as orphans; I will come to you."

These verses are loved by Muslims and they like to use them as their evidence. Did Muhammad live with the apostles of Jesus in the first century? ABSOLUTELY NOT. Muhammad was not there in the first century when Jesus' disciples received the Holy Spirit. Jesus told his disciples that he would not leave them as orphans. How could Muhammad, who came 600 years later, be with Jesus' disciples in the first century?

Eleventh Evidence:

John 14:26 says: "But the Advocate, the Holy Spirit, whom the Father will send in my name, will teach you all things and will remind you of everything I have said to you."

Muslims do not like this verse at all because Jesus clearly says who this Advocate is, it is the third person in the Holy Trinity. The Holy Spirit has all the attributes of the Father and the Son. Therefore, Muhammad fails miserably here. Muhammad was a sinner, whereas Jesus never committed a single sin.

Twelfth Evidence:

John 15:26 says: "When the Advocate comes, whom I will send to you from the Father—the Spirit of truth who goes out from the Father—he will testify about me."

Once again, this is the beauty of teaching in its context. We have read in the above verses that Jesus said who our Advocate is, and in more detail, HERE IN VERSE 26 Jesus says that the Advocate is the Holy Spirit.

Did Muhammad live during the time of Jesus' apostles and be their helper? ABSOLUTELY NOT, it is known that Muhammad came 600 years later.

Thirteenth Evidence:

John 16:13 says: "But when he, the Spirit of truth, comes, he will guide you into all the truth. He will not speak on his own; he will speak only what he hears, and he will tell you what is yet to come."

Muhammad fails here again because he did not speak or hear from God, Jehovah, but from Gabriel who he claimed was sent by Allah. Moreover, Muhammad did not prophesy about future events. MUHAMMAD FAILS AGAIN FOR THE THIRTEENTH TIME.

Fourteenth Evidence:

John 16:15 says: "All that belongs to the Father is mine. That is why I said the Spirit will receive from me what he will make known to you."

Jesus says that all that belongs to the Father is mine. Can any ordinary human claim that everything that belongs to God the Father is theirs? Surely Jesus is God. MOREOVER, Jesus says that the Holy Spirit will teach us about HIM/Jesus, whereas it is known that Muhammad did not teach about Jesus and Muhammad never said that Jesus has a Father. Therefore, the Holy Spirit cannot be Gabriel or a Muslim but is God with all the attributes of the Father and the Son.

Fifteenth Evidence:

JESUS GIVES THE HOLY SPIRIT TO HIS DISCIPLES

John 20:21-22 says: "21 Again Jesus said, 'Peace be with you! As the Father has sent me, I am sending you.' 22 And with that, he breathed on them and said, 'Receive the Holy Spirit.'"

THE ABOVE VERSES CLEARLY SHOW THAT JESUS GAVE THE HOLY SPIRIT TO HIS DISCIPLES AND NOT TO MUHAMMAD WHO WAS NOT YET BORN.

Therefore, today I have given more than fifteen pieces of evidence from the Gospel of John that Muhammad was

not the Spirit of Truth, and moreover, Gabriel was not the
Spirit of Truth.

TODAY I HAVE ANSWERED ABOUT THE
SPIRIT OF TRUTH WHOM JESUS WAS SPEAKING
ABOUT using the very verses Jesus used to talk about that
Spirit of Truth.

CHAPTER 08

WHO IS THE HOLY SPIRIT IN THE BIBLE AND QURAN?

The holy scriptures instruct us to acknowledge the oneness of God, affirming that He has no partners or equals. We read in the Quran:

"Say: He is Allah, the One, Allah the Eternal, He begets not, nor was He begotten, and there is none comparable to Him." (Surah 112:1-3)

Allah expresses the same concept in the Bible, as stated in:

"Hear, O Israel: The Lord our God, the Lord is one." (Deuteronomy 6:4)

The idea of there being three gods is strongly refuted by the holy scriptures. As we read in the Quran:

"They have certainly disbelieved who say, 'Allah is the third of three.' And there is no god except one God. And if they do not desist from what they are saying, there will surely afflict the disbelievers among them a painful punishment." (Surah 5:73)

"O People of the Scripture, do not commit excess in your religion or say about Allah except the truth. The Messiah, Jesus, the son of Mary, was but a messenger of Allah and His word which He directed to Mary and a soul [created at a command] from Him. So believe in Allah and His messengers. And do not say, 'Three'; desist - it is better for you. Indeed, Allah is but one God. Exalted is He above having a son. To Him belongs whatever is in the heavens and whatever is on the earth. And sufficient is Allah as Disposer of affairs." (Surah 4:171)

The concept that Allah is one and unique, incomparable to anything, is beyond doubt in the holy scriptures. The key issue here is to understand the nature of this oneness. The holy scriptures provide clear explanations about the nature of God. For example, in 1 John 5:8, we read:

"For there are three that testify in heaven: the Father, the Word, and the Holy Spirit, and these three are one."

Here, we see that unity in divinity is found in the three, meaning that unity in God cannot be understood without the three.

When we carefully examine the holy scriptures, we can discover that this concept of unity in plurality is clearly present. For example, during the creation of heaven and earth, we are told:

"Then God said, 'Let Us make man in Our image, according to Our likeness'" (Genesis 1:26)

From this verse, we see that God speaks in the singular form but indicates plurality, suggesting that He is not singular in the way humans understand, but one in His own nature, which is a plural unity. According to 1 John 5:8, this plurality is in the form of three persons.

This concept is also clearly present in the Quran, indicating that when God says He is one, it does not mean unity of a single person but rather more than one person. For example:

"And We created man from sounding clay, from mud moulded into shape." (Surah 15:26)

"We did not create the heavens and the earth and everything in between them except with truth and for a specified term…" (Surah 46:3)

This statement in the Quran clearly shows that God speaks in the plural form, indicating more than one person.

Islamic scholars explain that this statement of God does not mean more than one person except when God speaks in the form of exaltation. However, further investigation in the holy scriptures shows that this concept has no foundation and is merely human thought.

In the Holy Bible, we see that during creation, it is said:

"And the Spirit of God was hovering over the face of the waters..." (Genesis 1:2)

Thus, according to this verse, during creation, God was with His Spirit. So who is this Spirit of God?

We are told at the birth of the Prophet Jesus (pbuh) when the angel Gabriel (Jibril) was with Mary, he said:

"The Holy Spirit will come upon you, and the power of the Highest will overshadow you..." (Luke 1:35)

Jesus Himself, when He began His ministry, said:

"The Spirit of the Lord is upon Me..." (Luke 4:18)

From these scriptures, we see that indeed, Almighty God has His Holy Spirit, and this Holy Spirit is sent to His prophets as we read:

"Elizabeth was filled with the Holy Spirit, and she exclaimed with a loud cry..." (Luke 1:41-42)

"Zechariah, his father, was filled with the Holy Spirit and prophesied..." (Luke 1:67)

"And Jesus, full of the Holy Spirit, returned from the Jordan and was led by the Spirit in the wilderness" (Luke 4:1)

"And when Jesus was baptized, immediately he went up from the water, and behold, the heavens were opened to him, and he saw the Spirit of God descending like a dove and coming to rest on him" (Matthew 3:16)

The Holy Spirit is a living entity because one can blaspheme and contend with Him. The Spirit intercedes for us, and the Holy Spirit speaks.

"Then the Lord said, 'My Spirit shall not abide in man forever...'" (Genesis 6:3)

"But they rebelled and grieved His Holy Spirit..." (Isaiah 63:10)

"And do not grieve the Holy Spirit of God, by whom you were sealed for the day of redemption." (Ephesians 4:30)

"And whoever speaks a word against the Son of Man will be forgiven, but whoever speaks against the Holy Spirit will not be forgiven, either in this age or in the age to come." (Matthew 12:32)

The Holy Spirit of God intercedes for the people of God. The attribute of intercession is not of an inanimate thing. This means that the Holy Spirit is a living person.

"Likewise, the Spirit helps us in our weakness. For we do not know what to pray for as we ought, but the Spirit

Himself intercedes for us with groanings too deep for words." (Romans 8:26)

The Holy Spirit speaks. This attribute of speaking is that of a living person, not an inanimate object, or as some say, just a force.

"And the Spirit said to Philip, 'Go over and join this chariot.'" (Acts 8:29)

"Now there was a man in Jerusalem, whose name was Simeon, and this man was righteous and devout, waiting for the consolation of Israel, and the Holy Spirit was upon him. And it had been revealed to him by the Holy Spirit that he would not see death before he had seen the Lord's Christ." (Luke 2:25-26)

"For the Holy Spirit will teach you in that very hour what you ought to say." (Luke 12:12) (Emphasis is mine in these verses)

When Islamic scholars encounter the concept of the Spirit of God, they associate the Spirit of God with the Prophet Muhammad. For example, when they read in John 16:13:

"When the Spirit of truth comes, he will guide you into all the truth, for he will not speak on his own authority, but whatever he hears he will speak, and he will declare to you the things that are to come."

When Muslims read this verse, they believe it refers to the Prophet Muhammad (pbuh). However, we have seen that the Holy Spirit of God has the following attributes:

- He existed during creation (Genesis 1:2)

- He was present during the time of Noah (Genesis 6:3)

- He was present during the time of Moses (Isaiah 63:10)

- His role includes empowering the prophets and also interceding for us.

These attributes entirely exclude Muhammad from being the Holy Spirit or the Spirit of God. Muhammad was never sent to be our intercessor; instead, believers are commanded to pray for Muhammad. Indeed, God Himself is the intercessor for Muhammad.

"Indeed, Allah and His angels send blessings upon the Prophet. O you who have believed, ask [Allah to confer] blessing upon him and ask [Allah to grant him] peace." (Surah 33:56)

Allah sends blessings upon the Prophet, and thus believers are commanded to send blessings upon the Prophet. It is not the other way around where the Prophet blesses or intercedes for them. That is why when a Muslim mentions the name of the Prophet, they must conclude by saying "Salla Allahu alayhi wa sallam" (May Allah's blessings and peace be upon him). How can Allah pray for the Prophet? Which god would He pray to if He is the only One? Thus, we see that while God is one, He is not one in the way we understand. He is one in three living persons, and thus, in the matter of praying for the saints of God, one person can pray to another.

Who is the Holy Spirit in the Quran?

As we have seen in the Bible, God strengthened the Prophet Jesus with the Holy Spirit, and He performed many miracles.

"We gave Moses the Book and followed him up with a succession of messengers. We gave Jesus, the son of Mary, clear signs and strengthened him with the Holy Spirit. Is it that whenever there comes to you a messenger with what you yourselves desire not, you are puffed up with pride? Some you called impostors, and others you slay." (Surah 2:87)

"[The Day] when Allah will say, 'O Jesus, Son of Mary, remember My favor upon you and upon your mother when I supported you with the Holy Spirit, and you spoke to the people in the cradle and in maturity; and when I taught you writing and wisdom and the Torah and the Gospel; and when you designed from clay what was

like the form of a bird with My permission, then you breathed into it, and it became a bird with My permission; and you healed the blind and the leper with My permission, and when you brought forth the dead with My permission; and when I restrained the Children of Israel from [killing] you when you came to them with clear proofs, and those who disbelieved among them said, 'This is nothing but obvious magic.'" (Surah 5:110)

Muslims, to avoid the subject of the Holy Trinity in the Quran, say that the Holy Spirit mentioned in these verses is the Angel Gabriel. But when asked for the teaching that says the Holy Spirit is Gabriel, they cannot provide an answer. It is merely an assumption that Gabriel is the Holy Spirit. There are two verses in the Quran used by Islamic scholars to claim that Gabriel is the Holy Spirit. Let's examine these verses:

"Say, [O Muhammad], 'Whoever is an enemy to Gabriel - it is [none but] he who has brought the Qur'an down upon your heart, [O Muhammad], by permission of Allah, confirming that which was before it and as guidance and good tidings for the believers.'" (Surah 2:97)

"Say, the Pure Spirit has brought it down from your Lord in truth to make firm those who believe and as guidance and good tidings to the Muslims." (Surah 16:102)

So a Muslim, from these two verses, argues that "since 2:97 says the Quran was brought down by Gabriel, and 16:102 says the Quran was brought down by the Holy Spirit, we conclude that Gabriel is the Holy Spirit." This is a very weak argument and does not consider the overall meaning and logic of the scriptures. Nowhere in the Quran does Gabriel proclaim to the Prophet, "I, Gabriel, am the Holy Spirit," nor is there a hadith where the Prophet is informed that Gabriel is the Holy Spirit. Let's examine this issue in more depth.

How did the revelation (wahy) come to the Prophet?

We are told in the book called "Ar-Raheeq al-Makhtum" on page 109 about the forms of wahy to the Prophet (pbuh) as follows:

1. The true visions, which were the beginning of the revelation to the Prophet.

2. What the Angel used to cast into his thoughts and heart.

3. The Angel appearing to him in the form of a man.

4. The Prophet receiving wahy with the sound of a bell.

5. The Prophet seeing the Angel in his true form.

6. The direct words of Allah.

From this, we see that it is not right to take one way the Prophet received revelation and compare it to another verse that talks about the revelation to the Prophet. Doing so shows that the Prophet received revelation in only one way, denying the history of his life and the various ways he received revelation.

The Holy Spirit and His role in bringing revelation to the Prophet.

When you read Surah 16:102 carefully, without inserting the thoughts of the Islamic scholars, you will see it says:

"Say, the Holy Spirit has brought it down from your Lord in truth to make firm those who believe and as guidance and good tidings to the Muslims." (Surah 16:102)

In this verse, there is no mention of Gabriel, but the translator inserts his interpretation to make it seem that the Holy Spirit is Gabriel.

We have seen that the Prophet received revelation in various ways, and one of these ways is the Holy Spirit descending upon him, just as prophets receive revelation either through an angel being sent to them with a message or through inspiration from the Holy Spirit. It is clear that the Holy Spirit is distinguished from the angels, showing He is a different entity from the angels as we read in the Quran:

"The angels and the Spirit descend therein by permission of their Lord for every matter." (Surah 97:4)

Here, we see the angels descending with the revelation and the Holy Spirit descending with the revelation. Gabriel is the angel intended, and then there is the Holy Spirit. Both are mentioned together in connection with bringing revelation.

According to the Quran, the Holy Spirit enabled Mary, the mother of Jesus, to conceive.

As it is in the Bible, where the angel Gabriel came to Mary and brought the good news of her bearing a child by the power of the Holy Spirit (Luke 1:35 and Matthew 1:20), so it is in the Quran. We read:

"And Mary, the daughter of Imran, who guarded her chastity, so We breathed into her Our Spirit, and she believed in the words of her Lord and His scriptures and was of the devoutly obedient." (Surah 66:12)

"And she who guarded her chastity, so We breathed into her [garment] through Our Spirit, and We made her and her son a sign for the worlds." (Surah 21:91)

In these verses, it is impossible to say that Gabriel is the spirit breathed into Mary. The verse says, "We breathed into her Our Spirit." That is the Spirit of God, and thus, Jesus was born (pbuh).

The angel Gabriel in the Bible said, "Her pregnancy is by the power of the Holy Spirit" (Matthew 1:21).

It is neither possible nor logical that Gabriel is the Holy Spirit. For the verses in the Quran say, God breathed His Spirit into Mary's womb, and that Spirit became flesh.

According to the Quran, the Holy Spirit empowers believers to perform righteous deeds.

We understand that according to Islamic teachings, Gabriel is sent to the prophets, and his task is to bring revelation. This verse in the Quran, however, removes the assumption that Gabriel is the Holy Spirit.

"You will not find any people who believe in Allah and the Last Day making friendship with those who oppose Allah and His Messenger, even if they were their fathers or their sons or their brothers or their kindred. For such, He has written faith in their hearts, and strengthened them with a Spirit from Himself. And We will admit them to Gardens underneath which rivers flow, to dwell therein. Allah is well pleased with them, and they with Him. They are the Party of Allah. Verily, it is the Party of Allah that will be the successful." (Surah 58:22)

We are told that God strengthens believers "with a Spirit from Himself," and this is certainly not Gabriel's task. It is clear that believers, according to this verse, perform righteous deeds by the power of the Holy Spirit.

This understanding that believers are given power through the Holy Spirit is a key teaching of the Bible. Jesus promised to give His Holy Spirit to His followers to help them do the work He left for them:

"But you will receive power when the Holy Spirit has come upon you..." (Acts 1:8)

"If you then, who are evil, know how to give good gifts to your children, how much more will your heavenly Father give the Holy Spirit to those who ask Him!" (Luke 11:13)

Who is the Spirit of Truth according to the holy scriptures?

Muslims claim that the Prophet Muhammad is prophesied in the Bible as the Spirit of Truth. They say there is the Holy Spirit and also the Spirit of Truth. They claim that the Holy Spirit and the Spirit of Truth are two different entities. What is surprising in this claim is that the Spirit of Truth is not holy. Now, the question to ask is whether the Spirit of Truth is an unclean spirit because the opposite of holy is unclean.

According to the Scriptures, the Spirit that comes from God is the Holy Spirit, and He is the Spirit of Truth. He is called the Spirit of Truth to differentiate Him from the lying spirits that the Bible describes. Read these scriptures:

"Now the Spirit expressly says that in later times some will depart from the faith by devoting themselves to deceitful spirits and teachings of demons." (1 Timothy 4:1)

"And I saw three unclean spirits like frogs coming out of the mouth of the dragon, out of the mouth of the beast, and out of the mouth of the false prophet. These are demonic spirits…" (Revelation 16:13-14)

Therefore, Jesus called the Holy Spirit the Spirit of Truth to differentiate Him from these deceitful spirits misleading the world of faith in our time. Nevertheless, let's examine the verse that Muslims use, claiming it refers to Muhammad.

"But I tell you the truth, it is to your advantage that I go away, for if I do not go away, the Helper will not come to you. But if I go, I will send Him to you. And when He comes, He will convict the world concerning sin and righteousness and judgment: concerning sin, because they do not believe in Me; concerning righteousness, because I go to the Father, and you will see Me no longer; concerning judgment, because the ruler of this world is judged. I still have many things to say to you, but you cannot bear them now. When the Spirit of Truth comes, He will guide you into all the truth, for He will not speak on His own authority, but whatever He hears He will speak, and He will declare to you the things that are to come. He will glorify Me, for He will take what is Mine and declare it to you. All that the Father has is Mine; therefore I said that He will take what is Mine and declare it to you." (John 16:7-15)

According to this verse, Muslims claim that the one mentioned here is Muhammad because:

- The Spirit of Truth would convict the world concerning sin – Muhammad established the religion of Islam, warning people about evil and sin.

- The Spirit of Truth would convict the world concerning righteousness – Muhammad taught the religion of righteousness.

- The Spirit of Truth would convict the world concerning judgment – Muhammad taught Islam, which includes

laws and judgment.

The main issue is to examine whether the attributes of the Spirit of Truth fit Muhammad, and then to consider the matters of sin, righteousness, and judgment.

The attributes of the Spirit of Truth according to the words of Jesus.

Jesus Himself said about the Spirit of Truth:

"If you love Me, keep My commandments. And I will ask the Father, and He will give you another Helper to be with you forever, even the Spirit of Truth, whom the world cannot receive, because it neither sees Him nor knows Him. You know Him, for He dwells with you and will be in you." (John 14:15-17)

According to this verse, we discover the following:

- The Spirit of Truth is called the Helper and is given to believers when they love Jesus and keep His commandments. The question to ask is whether Muslims love Jesus and keep His commandments.

- The Spirit of Truth will be with us forever. The question to ask is whether Muhammad is with Muslims forever. No, Muhammad died on Monday, June 8, 632 AD, over 1400 years ago. (Abdalla Farsy, "Maisha ya Nabii Muhammad," p. 81)

- The Spirit of Truth is not seen by the world and is known only by believers. The question to ask is whether Muhammad was seen by unbelievers. Yes, Muhammad was seen by the opponents of Islam, and he fought battles with them.

"When they saw that he was not leaving, the 'elders' ordered the people of the town to stone him whenever they saw him, until he left. So, when the news spread, everyone came out with stones in their hands to hit the Prophet when they saw him. As soon as he appeared, they started throwing stones at him, not like children throwing ripe mangoes! He was soaked in blood from head to toe, and they did not let him rest even for a moment, following him for two miles. He was covered in blood from head to toe!" (Abdalla Farsy, "Maisha ya Nabii Muhammad," p. 30)

This story clearly shows that Muhammad was seen by the people of the world who were his opponents. The Spirit of Truth is not seen or known by those who do not know God. Most of all, they will deny His existence, claiming, "God has no partner."

The Spirit of Truth dwells within God's people.

"You, however, are not in the flesh but in the Spirit, if in fact the Spirit of God dwells in you. Anyone who does not have the Spirit of Christ does not belong to Him. But if Christ is in you, although the body is dead because of sin, the Spirit is life because of righteousness. If the Spirit of Him who raised Jesus from the dead dwells in you, He who raised Christ Jesus from the dead will also give life to your mortal bodies through His Spirit who dwells in you." (Romans 8:9-11)

Muhammad cannot enter and dwell within a person, making it impossible for him to be the Spirit of Truth.

According to John 16:7, the Holy Spirit is sent by Jesus: "But if I go, I will send Him to you." The fundamental question is that if Muhammad is a prophet and we recognize that prophets are sent by God, Jesus says He will send the Spirit of Truth. Since Muslims claim that this refers to Muhammad, then who will Jesus be to Muhammad? Clearly, since he is sent by Jesus, then Jesus is Muhammad's God, a fact that no Muslim can accept. If they do not accept this, then they should abandon this verse entirely, as it does not refer to Muhammad.

How does the Holy Spirit convict the world concerning sin, righteousness, and judgment?

We have seen that the prophets of God speak words from God led by the Holy Spirit.

"For prophecy never had its origin in the human will, but prophets, though human, spoke from God as they were carried along by the Holy Spirit." (2 Peter 1:21)

"It was revealed to them that they were not serving themselves but you, when they spoke of the things that have now been told you by those who have preached the gospel to you by the Holy Spirit sent from heaven." (1 Peter 1:12)

Therefore, when God's servants preach, rebuking sin and warning people of the coming judgment, this work is done by the Holy Spirit within them.

"Now to each one, the manifestation of the Spirit is given for the common good. To one there is given through the Spirit a message of wisdom, to another a message of knowledge by means of the same Spirit, to another faith by the same Spirit, to another gift of healing by that one Spirit, to another miraculous power, to another prophecy, to another distinguishing between spirits, to another speaking in different kinds of tongues, and to still another the interpretation of tongues. All these are the work of one and the same Spirit, and He distributes them to each one, just as He determines." (1 Corinthians 12:7-11)

God is One, but this unity of God does not mean unity as human understanding perceives. God is one in three living persons, and in this Trinity, He says He is incomparable, for no god or gods can have the attribute of being one God while simultaneously being three living persons. The Quran's rejection of the Trinity is because the Quraysh of Mecca had three gods worshipped in the form of idols. Muhammad forbade this pagan religion and prohibited people from worshipping Allah using these idol examples. We read in the Quran:

"So have you considered al-Lat and al-'Uzza? And Manat, the third - the other one? Is the male for you and for Him the female? That, then, is an unjust division." (Surah 53:19-22)

Muhammad complains that these gods have only female offspring! And that those who worship them have male offspring. Saying that the gods of the disbelievers have only female offspring is doing injustice to these gods, meaning they are not being treated fairly.

He continues by saying:

"These are not but [mere] names you have named them - you and your forefathers - for which Allah has sent down no authority. They follow not except assumption and what their souls desire, and there has already come to them from their Lord guidance." (Surah 53:23)

These are the three gods that the entire Quran refutes the belief of the disbelievers of Mecca. Jews and Christians were not worshipping three gods during Muhammad's time, nor is there a teaching of three gods in the Bible, except that GOD IS ONE WITH THREE LIVING PERSONS.

CHAPTER 09

CONFUSION: NOAH OF THE QURAN IS DIFFERENT FROM THE NOAH OF THE BIBLE

Muslims often claim that the Quran is a book that explains everything, is self-sufficient and has descended from Almighty God, while they criticize the Bible as not being from God. I will present two verses from the Bible and then two verses from the Quran, followed by a question.

WHEN DID THE FLOOD OCCUR ACCORDING TO THE BIBLE?

Genesis 7:6

"And Noah was six hundred years old when the flood of waters was upon the earth."

The Bible, which you say is not from God, states that Noah was six hundred (600) years old when the flood occurred. It also mentions Noah's age after the flood.

Genesis 9:28

"And Noah lived after the flood three hundred and fifty years."

HOW OLD WAS NOAH WHEN HE DIED?

Genesis 9:29

"And all the days of Noah were nine hundred and fifty years: and he died."

We are told by the Bible that Noah lived for three hundred and fifty (350) years after the flood and died at the age of nine hundred and fifty (950). These are the total years of Noah's life; he did not live beyond these years. Now let's look at the Quran and then ask the question.

WHEN DID THE FLOOD OCCUR ACCORDING TO THE QURAN?

Quran 29:14-15

14. "And We certainly sent Noah to his people, and he remained among them a thousand years minus fifty years, and the flood seized them while they were wrongdoers."

15. "But We saved him and the companions of the ship, and We made it a sign for the worlds."

MAIN TOPIC:

The Bible says the flood occurred when Noah was 600 years old. The Quran says the flood occurred when Noah was 950 years old, which matches the age of Noah at the time of his death according to the Bible. The Bible states that Noah lived for 350 years after the flood and died at 950 years old, matching the age given for Noah during the flood in the Quran.

QUESTIONS:

1. According to the Quran, Noah was 950 years old when the flood came. The Bible states he was 600 years old when the flood occurred and he died at 950 years old. According to the Quran, how many years did Noah live after those 950 years of the flood?

2. Did Noah die in the same year of the flood, at the age of 950 as stated during the flood in the Quran?

Note: The answers should come solely from the Quran, the book you claim is from God. If it is not sufficient, feel free to use magazines and journals.

CHAPTER 10

WHO IS GREATER BETWEEN APOSTLE PAUL AND MUHAMMAD ACCORDING TO THE SCRIPTURES?

LET'S COMPARE THESE TWO FIGURES

Muslims often blame and insult Apostle Paul, claiming he is a false apostle who corrupted the scriptures and started Christianity by declaring Jesus as God. These claims will be addressed in this study. Below are criteria to compare Paul and Muhammad to determine who is false and who is true according to the scriptures:

CRITERIA FOR COMPARISON:

1. Birth of Paul and Muhammad

2. Education of Paul and Muhammad

3. Religious beliefs of Paul and Muhammad

4. How Paul and Muhammad received their apostleship

5. Who performed miracles between Paul and Muhammad?

6. Does the Quran provide sufficient knowledge of prophets and apostles?

7. How Paul and Muhammad received their visions (wahyi)

8. The consequence of rejecting Apostle Paul

1. BIRTH OF PAUL AND MUHAMMAD

1. Birth of Paul:

Acts 22:3 states, "I am a Jew, born in Tarsus of Cilicia..." Historically, the city of Tarsus was under Roman rule, which is why Paul declared himself a Roman by birth (Acts 22:25-28). Paul said he was born in Tarsus, which was part of what was known as Asia Minor, now in modern-day Turkey. History shows that Paul was born around 10 AD.

Tarsus was famous for two main things: 1) High-level education, believed to have produced many scholars and philosophers, such as Athenodorus, a teacher of Emperor Augustus. 2) Tent-making craftsmanship, a trade Paul also knew and practiced to support himself and spread the Gospel without burdening anyone (Acts 18:1-3; 20:34; 2 Thessalonians 3:8). This is why Paul said he was from a significant city (Acts 21:39).

Paul was born into a distinguished lineage. Romans 11:1 states, "For I also am an Israelite, a descendant of Abraham, from the tribe of Benjamin." To understand the significance of this lineage, it is essential to know who Abraham was. Genesis 14:13 describes Abraham as a Hebrew, and he was blessed so that through him and his offspring, all nations would be blessed (Genesis 12:1-4; 22:15-18).

Paul also came from this lineage, as he stated in Philippians 3:4-5, "If someone else thinks they have reasons to put confidence in the flesh, I have more: circumcised on the eighth day, of the people of Israel, of the tribe of Benjamin, a Hebrew of Hebrews; in regard to the law, a Pharisee."

Hebrews are the Israelites who received the Law and were made sons and given a better covenant (Romans 9:4-5; Hebrews 7:22; 8:6). Benjamin was one of the 12 tribes of Israel.

2. Birth of Muhammad:

Muhammad was born in 570 AD in the city of Mecca, southeastern Arabia. His full name was Muhammad bin Abdullah bin Abd-Muttalib bin Hashim. The Quran (41:44) narrates that Muhammad was an Arab, and various Islamic books state that his tribe was Quraish.

Muhammad was born into a lineage that neither knew God nor any scripture. Quran 34:44 states, "And We did not give them (the Arabs) any scriptures which they might study, nor did We send them any warner before you."

Allah (as believed by Muslims) did not give the Arabs any scripture before the Quran. This means that from the time Muhammad was born until he reached 40 years old, neither he nor his fellow Arabs knew about the scriptures.

The commentary on Suratul Al-Furqan verse 43 includes, "The Arabs, in their ignorance of worshipping many gods, would worship anything that pleased them, even a nicely shaped pastry."

We have seen that Paul was born into a lineage of people who knew God, while Muhammad was born into a lineage of people who neither knew God nor scripture.

EDUCATION OF PAUL AND MUHAMMAD

1. Education of Paul:

Acts 22:3 states, "I am a Jew, born in Tarsus of Cilicia, but brought up in this city, educated at the feet of Gamaliel, strictly according to the law of our fathers, being zealous for God just as you all are today."

Who was Gamaliel in Israel? Acts 5:34 states, "But a Pharisee named Gamaliel, a teacher of the law, respected by all the people, stood up in the Council..."

Paul received higher education under this famous teacher of the law, Galatians 1:14 states, "I was advancing in Judaism beyond many of my own age among my people and was extremely zealous for the traditions of my fathers." This is why Paul could write 13 books under the power of the Holy Spirit (Galatians 6:11). Witnesses to his education include Apostle Peter and Governor Festus (2 Peter 3:15-17; Acts 26:24-25).

2. Education of Muhammad:

Quran 7:157 states, "Those who follow the Messenger, the unlettered prophet whom they find written in what they have of the Torah and the Gospel, who enjoins upon them what is right and forbids them what is wrong..."

Quran 62:2 states, "It is He who has sent among the unlettered a Messenger from themselves..."

In the book "The Life of Muhammad" by Sheikh Farsy, page 8, it says, "The Prophet grew up like the Quraish, without knowing how to read or write. No Quraish person could read or write."

Muhammad's lack of education is why he taught Muslims to use sand for ablution if water was unavailable (Quran 5:6). Another strange teaching of Muhammad is found in Mishkat Al-Masabih vol 11 page 152: "The Messenger of Allah (saw) said: 'If a fly falls into the vessel of any of you, let him dip it, for one of its wings has a disease and the other has the cure.'"

The Bible does not agree with such ignorance, as seen in Ezekiel 13:3: "Thus says the Lord God, 'Woe to the foolish prophets who follow their own spirit and have seen nothing!'"

4. RELIGIOUS BELIEFS OF PAUL AND MUHAMMAD

1. Paul:

He was in the Jewish religion, observing the Law and the teachings of the prophets before becoming a Christian (Galatians 1:13; Acts 26:4-5). Even after becoming a Christian, he continued to teach using the Law and the prophets. Acts 28:23 states, "They arranged to meet Paul on a certain day, and came in even larger numbers to the place where he was staying. He witnessed to them from morning till evening, explaining about the kingdom of God, and from the Law of Moses and from the Prophets he tried to persuade them about Jesus."

2. Muhammad:

He was a pagan Quraish who worshipped 360 gods, including the black stone in the Kaaba, before becoming a Muslim. These gods included Al-Lat, Al-Uzza, and Manat (Quran 53:16-23). See also "The Life of Muhammad," page 8.

5. HOW PAUL AND MUHAMMAD RECEIVED THEIR APOSTLESHIP

1. How Paul received apostleship:

Paul was given apostleship directly by Jesus on his way to Damascus. Jesus appeared to him and instructed him on what to do (Acts 9:1-8). Jesus confirmed Paul's apostleship through His disciple Ananias, who was told in a vision to meet Paul (Acts 9:11-15). Ananias also baptized Paul (Acts 9:18).

Paul responded to his apostolic call by Jesus, saying in Romans 1:1, "Paul, a servant of Christ Jesus, called to be an apostle and set apart for the gospel of God."

Did Paul fulfill this apostolic mission of spreading the gospel to nations and standing before kings and the Israelites? Yes. The countries Paul preached in include Arabia, Athens (Greece), Damascus (Syria), Rome (Italy), Jerusalem (Israel), Spain, Ephesus, Galatia, Corinth, Philippi, Thessalonica, Crete, and more. Everywhere he went, he faced challenges that led him to stand before kings, governors, and the Israelites (Galatians 1:17; Acts 9:19-20, 26-29; 17:16-22; 18:19; 19:35; 28:16-30; Romans 15:24-28).

2. How Muhammad received apostleship:

In "The Life of Prophet Muhammad" by Sheikh Abdallah Farsy, pages 11-13, 81, it states:

One day during the month of Ramadan on the 17th Monday, Muhammad, aged 40 and a half, saw a man standing before him without knowing where he came from. The man said, "Read," but Muhammad replied that he could not read because he had never learned to read. The man then embraced him tightly and repeated the command. After the third time, the man said, "Read in the name of your Lord who created..." and recited Surah 96. Muhammad then recited it back. The man then vanished. Muhammad returned home in fear, and his wife Khadija covered him, thinking he had a fever. She listened to his story and reassured him, saying there was nothing to fear.

Khadija then went to her cousin, Waraqa bin Naufal, and told him what happened. Waraqa said that it was Gabriel who had come to Muhammad, the same angel who had come to Moses and Jesus. Waraqa then confirmed Muhammad's apostleship.

In "The Great Deeds of Muhammad," it says:

When Muhammad left the cave and headed home after being embraced by the unknown man, he was trembling and hallucinating, fearing for his sanity and that he might be possessed by demons. His wife Khadija comforted him and took him to Waraqa bin Naufal, a Christian priest, who confirmed Muhammad's apostleship.

So, Muhammad's apostleship was confirmed by Waraqa and Khadija. Without them, Muhammad would not have been recognized as an apostle.

DOUBTS ABOUT MUHAMMAD'S APOSTLESHIP:

- Muhammad was embraced by an unknown figure.

- Muhammad admitted he was played with by demons, affecting his sanity.

- Muhammad's apostleship was predicted by his wife and a Catholic priest, Waraqa bin Naufal.

6. DID PAUL OR MUHAMMAD PERFORM MIRACLES?

Paul:

Acts 19:11 states, "God did extraordinary miracles through Paul, so that even handkerchiefs and aprons that had touched him were taken to the sick, and their illnesses were cured, and the evil spirits left them."

Muhammad:

Muhammad did not perform miracles and was affected by witchcraft (sorcery). Quran 29:50 states, "And they say, 'Why are not signs sent down to him from his Lord?' Say, 'The signs are only with Allah, and I am only a plain warner.'"

7. HOW PAUL AND MUHAMMAD RECEIVED VISIONS (WAHYI)

Paul:

Acts 16:10 states, "After Paul had seen the vision, we got ready at once to leave for Macedonia, concluding that God had called us to preach the gospel to them."

Acts 18:9 states, "One night the Lord spoke to Paul in a vision: 'Do not be afraid; keep on speaking, do not be silent.'"

Acts 26:19 states, "So then, King Agrippa, I was not disobedient to the vision from heaven."

Muhammad:

In the book "The Trustworthy One," volumes 1-2, Muhammad described his revelations:

"Sometimes the revelation comes to me like the ringing of a bell, and that is the hardest on me, then it leaves me, and I understand what was said."

8. CONSEQUENCES OF INSULTING APOSTLE PAUL

2 Peter 3:15-18 states, "Bear in mind that our Lord's patience means salvation, just as our dear brother Paul also wrote you with the wisdom that God gave him. He writes the

same way in all his letters, speaking in them of these matters. His letters contain some things that are hard to understand, which ignorant and unstable people distort, as they do the other Scriptures, to their own destruction. Therefore, dear friends, since you have been forewarned, be on your guard so that you may not be carried away by the error of the lawless and fall from your secure position. But grow in the grace and knowledge of our Lord and Savior Jesus Christ. To him be glory both now and forever! Amen."

Romans 2:16 states, "This will take place on the day when God judges people's secrets through Jesus Christ, as my gospel declares."

CONCLUSION

Those who reject Apostle Paul and the gospel he preached are called lawless, sinners, unstable, and distorters of Scripture, and their end is condemnation according to the Bible.

CHAPTER 11

THE APOSTLESHIP OF PAUL ACCORDING TO THE QURAN AND HADITH

The Beginning of Paul's Apostleship:

In Numbers 12:6, God explains how prophets and apostles receive revelations from Him. Did Paul possess this qualification of receiving revelations?

We read in Acts 16:9, "During the night Paul had a vision..."

Did God specify to whom Paul was sent?

Acts 9:15, "But the Lord said to Ananias, 'Go! This man is my chosen instrument to proclaim my name to the Gentiles and their kings and to the people of Israel.'"

Acts 13:2, "While they were worshiping the Lord and fasting, the Holy Spirit said, 'Set apart for me Barnabas and Saul for the work to which I have called them.'"

How does Paul himself testify about his apostleship?

Galatians 1:1, "Paul, an apostle—sent not from men nor by a man, but by Jesus Christ and God the Father, who raised him from the dead."

Colossians 1:1, "Paul, an apostle of Christ Jesus by the will of God, and Timothy our brother."

Here, Paul helps us answer the question of our topic, stating he is an "apostle of God."

THE APOSTLESHIP OF PAUL ACCORDING TO THE QURAN AND HADITH

First, let me remind you of the articles of faith in Islam (Swifat ul I'iman mufaswalu):

1. Belief in God

2. Belief in the angels of God

3. Belief in the books of God

4. Belief in His messengers

5. Belief in the Day of Judgment

6. Belief in divine decree (Qadar), the good and bad thereof

For the purposes of this discussion, I will focus on the fourth article: Belief in the messengers of God.

In Islamic belief, there are about 124,000 prophets. Among them, only 25 are mentioned specifically in the Quran as revealed to Prophet Muhammad (S.A.W.), as stated in Surah 4:164:

"We have already sent messengers before you. Among them are those [whose stories] We have related to you, and among them are those [whose stories] We have not related to you. And God spoke to Moses directly."

"And say: We believe in God and what was revealed to us and what was revealed to Abraham, Ishmael, Isaac, Jacob, and the descendants, and what was given to Moses and Jesus and what was given to the prophets from their Lord. We make no distinction between any of them, and to Him, we have submitted."

This verse instructs Muslims to believe in all previous prophets, including those given to the descendants of Jacob, and all other prophets not mentioned in the Quran.

Paul himself stated he is a descendant of Jacob:

"...I am an Israelite myself, a descendant of Abraham, from the tribe of Benjamin." (Romans 11:1)

Benjamin was a son of Jacob. Therefore, it is evident that Surah 2:136 requires belief in all preceding prophets, including Paul, and all prophets mentioned in the Torah, Psalms, and Gospel.

It appears that Prophet Muhammad was not informed about a vast majority of the prophets. Most of the prophets mentioned in the Quran are also mentioned in the Bible. Hence, when Muslims seek more knowledge about prophets, they should heed God's command to Muhammad in Surah 10:94:

"So if you are in doubt, [O Muhammad], about that which We have revealed to you, then ask those who have been reading the Scripture before you..."

It is surprising to see that some Muslims today reject the apostleship of Paul, a stance taken without considering the Quran and the teachings of Prophet Muhammad (S.A.W.). It seems those who oppose this lack sufficient knowledge of the Quran and Islam itself.

Let's examine this issue using the Quran, Hadith, and various Islamic scholars' commentaries.

We read in the Quran 36:13-14 that God reminds the Prophet about the people of a certain town to whom He sent "messengers." Many Quranic commentators, including Sheikh Balwani and Yusuf Ali, identify this town as Antioch. Ibn Kathir further explains that the names of these messengers were John, Simon, and Paul.

It is clear that this opposition to Paul within Islam is very recent. Hadiths show that early Muslims did not have an issue with Paul's apostleship.

In the book written by Ibn Hisham, "Sirat Nabawiyat," volume 4, page 140, there is a section where Prophet Muhammad lists the disciples of Jesus and their assigned regions. Among them, he mentions that Paul was sent to the Romans.

My fellow Muslims, rejecting Paul's apostleship is equivalent to rejecting faith, the religion itself, and the Quran, ultimately opposing God. Therefore, rejecting Paul's apostleship is an extreme act of disbelief that God cannot tolerate.

Satan is very cunning and has many ways to mislead people. Many think they are defending the religion by opposing Paul's apostleship, but in reality, they are undermining it. AVOID FALLING INTO THIS TRAP.

Having examined the evidence of Paul's apostleship in the Holy Bible, let's turn to the Holy Quran for further confirmation.

THE APOSTLESHIP OF PAUL ACCORDING TO THE HOLY QURAN

To begin, let me remind Muslims that Islam has the following attributes (Swifat ul I'iman mufaswalu):

1. Faith in God.

2. Faith in the angels of God.

3. Faith in the books of God.

4. Faith in the messengers of God.

5. Faith in the divine decree (Qadar), the good and the bad thereof.

6. Faith in the Day of Judgment.

Today's topic focuses on the faith in messengers. Muslims believe there are about 124,000 prophets. Among them, only 25 were specifically mentioned to Prophet Muhammad (S.A.W.). As we read in Surah An-Nisa 164:

"And We sent messengers We have mentioned to you before and messengers We have not mentioned to you. And Allah spoke to Moses directly."

This means Muhammad had very limited knowledge of prophets, only about 0.0002%. This is the extent of all Muslims' knowledge regarding prophets. However, Allah had already directed the Prophet to where he could get more enlightenment, saying:

Surah Yunus 10:94, "So if you are in doubt about what We have revealed to you, then ask those who have been reading the Scripture before you. The truth has certainly come to you from your Lord, so never be among the doubters."

Therefore, for information about prophets, almost all the prophets mentioned to Muhammad are in the Bible. As stated in the first part of our discussion today, we affirm Paul's apostleship to Muslims.

Nevertheless, if you carefully read the Quran, you will find that it narrates about Paul comprehensively.

Examine this verse:

Surah Ya-Sin 36:13-14, "And present to them an example: the people of the city, when the messengers came to it. When We sent to them two but they denied them, so We strengthened them with a third, and they said, 'Indeed, we are messengers to you.'"

This verse recounts the story of God's messengers. Commentators and scholars like Sheikh Balwani and Yusuf Ali interpret this verse, identifying the city as Antioch. Ibn Kathir in his tafsir explains that these messengers were John, Simon, and Paul.

Thanks to Ibn Kathir, he says:

"It was narrated from Ibn Jurayj from Wahb bin Sulayman, narrated by Shu'ayb Al-Jaba'i, 'The names of the two messengers first sent were Simon and John, and the name of the third was Paul. And the city was Antioch.' They said (to the people of the city), 'Indeed, we have been sent to you as messengers,' meaning 'Messengers from Allah who created you and commands you to worship Him alone.' Qatada said they were messengers of the Messiah Jesus son of Mary (a.s.) sent to the people of Antioch. They said, 'You are but human beings like us,' indicating their disbelief."

Thus, it is clear that the idea of rejecting Paul is a recent fabrication. Early Muslims, scholars, and religious leaders did not have this notion of rejecting Paul.

PAUL'S APOSTLESHIP ACCORDING TO THE HADITH

After seeing the evidence from the holy books regarding Paul's apostleship, let us now turn to the Hadith of Prophet Muhammad. Why refer to the Hadith? Because of the guidance provided by Allah in the Quran itself.

Surah An-Nisa 59, "O you who have believed, obey Allah and obey the Messenger and those in authority among you. And if you disagree over anything, refer it to Allah and the Messenger if you should believe in Allah and the Last Day. That is the best [way] and best in result."

In the book "Sirat Nabawiya" written by Ibn Hisham, who was a student of Ibn Ishaq, in volume 4, page 140, Muhammad lists the names of Jesus' disciples, dividing them into two groups: those who followed Jesus during his lifetime and those who followed after his ascension. Muhammad explains each disciple's mission and the regions they were sent to, noting that Paul was sent to Rome.

Thanks to Ibn Hisham:

"The names of Jesus' apostles:

Ibn Ishaq said: Among those sent by Jesus the Messiah (peace be upon him) of the apostles and followers who were after him on the earth were: Peter the apostle, along with Paul. Paul was one of the followers and not one of the apostles. He was sent to Rome. Andrew and Matthias were

sent to the land where people eat others, and Thomas was sent to the land of Babel in the east. Philip was sent to Carthage, which is Africa; John to Ephesus, the village of the companions of the cave; James to Jerusalem, which is Aelia, the village of the Holy House, and Bartholomew to Arabia, which is the land of Hijaz. Simon to the land of Berbers, and Judas, who was not one of the apostles, was made instead of Judas."

It is surprising that despite this significant evidence, some modern Muslims (especially activists) have decided to ignore this truth and start misleading people, either deliberately or out of ignorance. The question is, for whose benefit are they doing this?

My Muslim friend, I warn you that Satan is cunning; he will always come with tricks, using false teachers who pretend to defend religion but are actually its greatest destroyers. Allah says in the Quran to tell Muslims:

Surah Al-Baqarah 136, "Say, 'We have believed in Allah and what has been revealed to us and what has been revealed to Abraham and Ishmael and Isaac and Jacob and the descendants and what was given to Moses and Jesus and what was given to the prophets from their Lord. We make no distinction between any of them, and we are Muslims [in submission] to Him.'"

You see that Allah instructs Muslims not only to believe in the 25 prophets mentioned in the Quran but also in what was revealed to Jacob's descendants. PAUL IS ALSO A DESCENDANT OF THE PROPHET JACOB. Furthermore, Allah commands Muslims to believe in other prophets. PAUL IS ALSO ONE OF THE OTHER PROPHETS.

Thus, rejecting Paul is rejecting faith, rejecting the Quran, and ultimately rejecting Allah Himself. THIS IS EXTREME DISBELIEF.

Is there any hadith of the Prophet where he warned his companions or Muslims about Paul's teachings? No, instead, we see Muhammad himself quoting Paul's teachings and calling them a message from Allah:

Narrated by Abu Huraira, the Messenger of Allah (s.a.w) said: "Allah said, 'I have prepared for My righteous servants what no eye has seen, what no ear has heard, and what no human heart has conceived.'"

Therefore, rejecting Paul's apostleship has no basis in the teachings of the holy books. It is a distortion by religious teachers seeking their own interests.

CHAPTER 12

HAS ISLAM IMPROVED AND BECOME BETTER
THAN CHRISTIANITY?

Does Muhammad fulfill and complete the mission and ministry of Christ? Muhammad emphatically answers 'yes.'

The core theology of Islam teaches that since Allah sent Gabriel with the Quran to Muhammad, the Messenger of Allah, both Muhammad and the Quran fulfill and complete the mission and ministry of Christ and the New Testament. Muhammad seems to acknowledge the significance of the Bible (Surah 4:47; 4:136; 4:163; 5:44-48; 5:82-83; 6:92, 154), but Christianity and the New Testament are supposed to submit to Islam and the Quran, the new and superior revelation.

Surah 5:15-16 expresses Muhammad's perspective using a metaphor. Within the context of Muhammad's distortion of Christian teachings that Jesus is the Son (v. 17) and his claims that the Jews are cursed (v. 13), this passage in the Quran (among others) states that Christians (and Jews) have been walking in darkness until Muhammad came:

5:15 "O People of the Book [Jews and Christians]... indeed, there has come to you from Allah a light and a clear Book [Quran] 16 by which Allah guides those who pursue His pleasure to the ways of peace and brings them out from darkness into light, by His permission, and guides them to a straight path." (Haleem) (compare with 4:157).

A Christian today with knowledge of the Bible will immediately recognize the metaphor of light. Jesus says He was sent from heaven as the light of the world, and Christians have crossed from darkness into light (John 1:4-5, 8:12, 9:5, 12:46; 1 Peter 2:9). However, now, Muhammad claims that Christians have been living in darkness, and he has come to clarify matters for them as if things were muddled. The Quran offers guidance on the "straight path," a theme repeated several times in Islamic scriptures (e.g., Surah 1) and "clarifies matters." Verse 16 is one of the verses a Muslim might consider when asserting that Islam is a religion of peace. But is it true?

A dedicated Christian with knowledge of the Bible cannot in any way believe that Islam is superior; how can we resolve this entrenched tension? Should we ignore it? Considering recent events like the terrorist attacks in the USA (September 11, 9/11), this is no longer possible. Should we pretend to believe that all religions are equal? But this forces us to deny some fundamental, non-negotiable doctrines that all religions have and that cannot be reconciled. Therefore, should we debate these irreconcilable teachings?

Discussing theological issues like the Trinity has its place in conversations between Muslims and Christians, but neither side can claim to prove their points through simple observation. The Quran consistently declares the oneness of God, while the New Testament firmly asserts that Jesus is God and the Holy Spirit is a person. Therefore, we set one sacred scripture against another, and to break this endless tension, we must use other methods. (For more reliable information on the New Testament, visit this site; for inherent problems with the Quran, go here.)

Since Muhammad opposes Christ and Christianity as true, we Christians must respond. How would Jesus respond? As it turns out, Jesus gave us clear teachings on how to assess a prophet who comes after him in history, especially one who claims to be greater than Jesus: assess their fruits.

In the context of the Sermon on the Mount, Christ spoke to the crowds, most of whom were not theologians or very few but were mostly lowly farmers. In Matthew 7:15-20,

Christ uses unmistakable language on how to recognize the truth about prophets:

7:15 "Beware of false prophets, who come to you in sheep's clothing but inwardly are ravenous wolves. 16 You will recognize them by their fruits. Are grapes gathered from thorn bushes or figs from thistles? 17 So, every healthy tree bears good fruit, but the diseased tree bears bad fruit. 18 A healthy tree cannot bear bad fruit, nor can a diseased tree bear good fruit. 19 Every tree that does not bear good fruit is cut down and thrown into the fire. 20 Thus, you will recognize them by their fruits."

In today's Western world, where millions of people prefer to appease Islam rather than challenge it, this passage might seem intolerant. But in these verses, Christ understands the danger. Claims to religious truths have come into the world in large numbers, almost every second, and these claims are not trivial; people's lives are at stake. Therefore, the cost of appeasement, especially since 9/11, is too high.

Furthermore, it is Muhammad who claimed to be greater than Christ and that his new religion is superior to Christianity. He is the one who initiated the opposition. Therefore, over 600 years before Muhammad's arrival, Christ responded to him and many others who call themselves prophets spreading across the Mediterranean Sea through the test of fruits.

To illustrate, let's say I claim that my way is better than yours. Then I can prove my verbal claims with visible actions. My conduct will be better than yours because my actions speak louder than words. For example, if the founder of a religion says that husbands in my community are allowed to beat their wives (Surah 4:34), but you as a founder say that husbands in your community are not allowed to beat their wives, can my claimed superiority stand in real life? I am setting a bad example in practice, but you are not. What I do is fail the fruit test. That is, my fruit or actual conduct or actions are rotten. Therefore, Jesus is entirely correct in using this simple analogy for his followers to scrutinize the claims of prophets who would come after him. "You will recognize them by their fruits" (Matthew 7:16).

We can see the essence of Muhammad's objection and Christ's fruit test through a simple if-then (cause/effect) logical argument. This method is known as "modus tollens" or denying the consequent (the "then" part).

(1) If A, then B. If Islam has improved and become better than Christianity, then this improvement would be evident in real and relevant ways.

(2) Not B. But this improvement is not evident in real and relevant ways.

(3) Therefore, not A. Therefore, Islam has not improved and become better than Christianity.

Now we can easily defend each statement.

(1) If Islam has improved and become better than Christianity, then this improvement would be evident in real and relevant ways.

We have already defended this statement in the preceding section. Examining the lives and actions of the founder of Christianity and the founder of Islam is the first and best way to break the endless tension between these two opposing religions, as we can see their behaviors and actions here on earth. You will recognize them by their fruits.

(2) But these changes are not evident in real and relevant ways.

Defending this statement with tangible evidence directly counters Muhammad's claims against Christ and undeniably demonstrates that the fruit of Muhammad is bad, while the fruit of Christ is healthy and ripe.

The following list has been compiled from an article on this website, which is the basis of this discussion. If the reader believes that the actual deeds of Muhammad and the verses from the Quran mentioned are taken out of context or are unclear, then they should visit the other provided sources. These morally questionable actions indeed occurred within

Muhammad's community, and Muhammad, in his Quran, endorses such cruelty. Also, to see the Quranic verses in multiple translations, readers should go here and type the references, such as 24:2 (24 is the Surah, and 2 is the verse). Ignore the Arabic chapter headings quoted in different formats and type the numbers only.

Muhammad gives nicknames to his weapons and calls himself "the annihilator."

Christ never owned weapons because he never engaged in warfare.

In his Quran, Muhammad orders that adulterers be flogged with a hundred lashes (Surah 24:2). Reliable hadiths (sayings and actions of Muhammad outside the Quran) mandate stoning them.

Christ forgave the woman caught in adultery. Those gathered to stone her dropped their stones and left. She remained, crying until Jesus told her to go and sin no more (John 8:1-11).

In his Quran, Muhammad permits men to beat their wives (Surah 4:34).

Neither Christ nor the writers of the New Testament ever allowed or practiced this.

In his Quran, Muhammad orders that the hands of thieves, whether male or female, be cut off (Surah 5:38).

Christ never advocated this. Apostle Paul stated that thieves should work with their hands, not have them cut off, so they might have something to share with those in need (Ephesians 4:28). In this (and many other aspects), Paul surpasses Muhammad.

Muhammad killed poets and political opponents.

Christ never killed any of his enemies, not even poets (even the bad ones).

In his Quran, Muhammad commands the death penalty or the cutting off of hands and feet for those who fight or cause corruption in the land (Surah 5:33).

Christ, the Prince of Peace, died for the sins of the world so that "corruption" and "fighting" might end.

Muhammad married Aisha, a girl who had not yet reached puberty, and consummated the marriage when she was still very young. For detailed evidence on this extraordinary family practice of Muhammad, even for 7th century Arabia, readers should look at this article. The Quran itself permits such marriages, which are not lawful for other Muslims (Surah 65:4).

Christ never did this, nor did he tell others to do so.

In his Quran, Muhammad promises an enticing paradise "full of virgins" for martyrs who lose their lives in holy wars (Surah 44:51-56, 52:17-29, 55:46-78, 61:10, 4:74, 9:111).

Christ's "martyrdom" on the cross means that Christians do not have to die in holy wars to gain assurance of entering heaven. They only need to believe in Jesus.

Muhammad unjustly killed nearly 600 Jewish men and enslaved their women and children. This brutality is celebrated in the Quran (Surah 33:25-27).

Christ was a Jew and loved his people. Moreover, he loves all people of the world—even those who worship many gods whom Muhammad killed—and redeems them through his death, burial, and resurrection. He was not sent to kill people.

Muhammad initiated his religious crusade in 630 AD with 30,000 fighters against the Byzantines—who did not show up (Surah 9:29).

Christ never did this. What medieval Europeans did in his name is not the foundation of Christianity. Only Jesus and the New Testament form the foundation, and they did not endorse holy wars. Muhammad, on the other hand, is the foundation of Islam and initiated holy wars against Byzantine Christians, endorsing and participating in many such wars.

Surah 5:16, quoted in the introduction of this article, emphatically states that Islam is a religion of peace. However, this list directly contradicts that assertion. Actions speak louder than words. Therefore, Islam is not a religion of peace; see this website. Again, if the reader believes that these points are taken out of context, they should click on the link above and then visit the other provided sources for each point.

Christians will recognize prophets by their fruits. To put it plainly, Muhammad, the self-proclaimed messenger and prophet (Surah 3:144), has utterly failed the practical fruit test. On the other hand, Christ, the Son of God (Matthew 3:16-17), has passed with perfect success.

(3) Therefore, Islam has not improved and become better than Christianity.

This conclusion follows directly and logically.

For people who are neutral and ready to hear arguments, real-life issues such as wife-beating, flogging adulterers, and marrying prepubescent girls are enough to make a decision. Practical actions and policies cannot be ignored unless people choose to close their eyes and refuse to see how obviously wrong things are, or perhaps if a prophet has a large army to enforce his actions on the "weak" followers of the "imperfect" previous religion.

And this brings us back to theoretical teachings, using myself and the reader as examples. Before discussing theoretically based doctrines like the nature of God, as a follower of a religion, I must pass the fruit test. Suppose it is my practice to kill polytheists in massively lethal wars, rather than convert them by preaching alone or let them live if they refuse to convert (Surah 9:4-5). On the other hand, it is not your practice to kill polytheists, but rather convert them by preaching alone and let them live if they refuse to convert. In these circumstances, I fail the practical and visible fruit test, but you pass. Therefore, I lose my credibility on other claims about the nature of God and other theoretical teachings that cannot be observed. It becomes evident that either I am serving myself or, worse—serving a false god. You, on the other hand, have practical and workable ideas, so you deserve to be listened to.

Similarly, Muhammad's failure in his opposition to Christ can be explained through another if-then argument, this time using the logical principle called modus ponens or affirming the antecedent (the "if" clause).

(4) If A, then B. If Islam has not improved and become better than Christianity in practical and observable ways, it logically follows that it has not improved and become better than Christianity in theoretical and abstract ways.

(5) A is affirmed. Islam has not improved and become better than Christianity in practical and observable ways.

(6) B is affirmed. Therefore, Islam has not improved and become better than Christianity in theoretical and abstract ways.

The first two premises can be easily defended.

(4) If Islam has not improved and become better than Christianity in practical and observable ways, it logically follows that it has not improved and become better than Christianity in theoretical and abstract ways.

Muhammad is a representation of Islam as he was the channel through which Allah revealed the superior religion, so we use him again to measure Islam. The fruit test states that if a prophet fails it, then his more abstract claims are suspect. In the context of the secular world, this test is much harsher because all humans have flaws. A physicist is allowed to discuss abstract ideas about space and time even if his life is messed up or full of sins. But in a religious context, especially when one religious leader (Muhammad) claims to be better than another leader (Christ), this test is crucial and unavoidable.

Moreover, factual evidence confirms Muhammad's failure in theoretical ideas. For example, it is a verifiable fact that the New Testament is reliable, whereas the Quran has its share of problems (for more on this, see these pages here and here). Also, it is verifiable that Muhammad was not educated in higher thought processes. What he did was incorporate a mixture of ideas prevalent along trade routes into his Quran (such as the illogical idea denying Christ's crucifixion in Surah

4:157), claiming it was divine revelation from Allah. Therefore, in clear and observable ways, Muhammad was not improving Christianity (and Judaism), but rather distorting these two preceding religions. Hence, historical truth confirms that he could be wrong on theoretical teachings—he did not understand what he was talking about.

(5) Islam has not improved and become better than Christianity in practical and observable ways.

After reviewing the list in the second argument, any objective seeker with reasoning and understanding, whose thoughts are not clouded by a lifelong devotion to Islam, will conclude that Muhammad has failed the fruit test in practical, observable, and relevant ways.

(6) Therefore, Islam has not improved and become better than Christianity in theoretical and abstract ways.

This conclusion follows logically and clearly.

Using the extensive list of major differences between Christ and Muhammad in the second argument, why would neutral and open-minded individuals consider the abstract teachings of Muhammad that deny the Trinity or the divinity of Christ (Surah 2:116, 6:101, 4:171, 5:73) or accept without question the corruption of the Quran (unless he has a large army)? Neutral and open-minded fruit inspectors can see that his claimed divinely inspired book is questionable because of his questionable life and because it is filled with injustices.

Indeed, neutral and open-minded individuals have every right to prefer the true and gentler Book of Christ, even if

it is said to have "errors," over Muhammad's Scriptures that claim to be "perfect" but are excessive. First, Muhammad must show us his exemplary life before he is allowed to preach higher theology or before we accept his abstract revelations as true.

For ordinary Christians, especially the first followers Jesus was teaching in the Sermon on the Mount, who were first-century Israeli farmers, Christ said that by the fruit of a prophet, his followers would know them. Once the fruit of a prophet is bad, or the tree starts bearing bad fruit, they do not need to examine his abstract claims. Such a person is a false prophet—strong words for sure, but these are the words of Christ (Matthew 7:15).

Three questions: Does this failure to pass the fruit test render the entire debate pointless? If Christian and Islamic theologians in a conference room want to discuss the Trinity, they are free to do so—although it is doubtful how far they can go. Their discussions are purely academic. However, they should not expect millions upon millions of Bible-literate Christians worldwide to feel compelled to debate these issues. But even if they wish to debate abstract theology, they are free to do so. Muslims should not be surprised, however, if at the end of the day these Christians do not accept Muhammad and his revelations as true because Christ has already told his followers what to look for: good fruit (Matthew 7:15-20). Muhammad lived a controversial life preserved in his Quran, which claims to be eternal and infallible, so Christians are allowed to doubt the Quran on abstract matters.

Is the relationship between practical and abstract matters self-contradictory? Christ in Matthew 7:15-20 suggests that this relationship is indeed not self-contradictory. Again, if Muhammad was not correct about practical matters such as beating wives, flogging adulterers, initiating military assaults of holy wars, killing poets and enemies, and promising his warriors gardens full of virgins if they die in holy wars, why should Christians listen to Muhammad on abstract matters, especially since the New Testament consistently affirms, for example, that Christ is God and the Holy Spirit is a person? And most importantly, why would Christians want to convert to Islam, given Muhammad's questionable conduct?

Are there no good qualities (fruit) attributed to Muhammad? Even the greatest failure in the fruit test can have some good qualities. The founder of a movement must show some level of gentleness if he wants his community to endure. However, good qualities do not beat and harm others. Conversely, bad behavior harms and hurts others. The overall picture of Muhammad's life in Medina (622-632 AD) shows him fighting wars against polytheists (conquering Mecca), against Jews (exiling and killing them), and against Christians (initiating holy wars). In the ten years he lived there, he embarked on, sent, or initiated seventy-four military assaults, ranging from peaceful negotiations (very few compared to violent assaults), to raiding parties, to the conquest of Mecca with 10,000 fighters, to holy wars against the Byzantines with 30,000 fighters (who did not show up). No one can clean up this dark picture by highlighting some good traits.

Therefore, Muhammad does not complete or fulfill the mission and ministry of Christ—quite the opposite, since Christ came into the world to show God's love. Indeed, Muhammad and Islam are a misrepresentation of Christ and Christianity, and the Quran is worse than the New Testament when viewed through examinable matters.

Has Islam positioned itself to be better than Christianity? Judging by observable evidence, the answer is a resounding no. Muhammad has utterly failed the simple fruit test.